Thirty-One Reasons to Praise

A 31-Day Devotion & Journal

Because life gets rough sometimes...

Melanie N. Lee

BY THEIR FRUITS YOU WILL KNOW THEM

NEW STANDARD

*To the rough moments that forced me to
search for reasons to praise.*

CONTENTS

Introduction

Rejoice in the Lord always. Again I will say, rejoice.

-Philippians 4:4

Expressing admiration, giving a warm approval, showing respect and gratitude. These are all words that define praise.

In Philippians 4:4 we are encouraged to have praise on our lips at all times. Yes, this includes those moments that don't feel very praiseworthy. If we can find one thing to praise God for in the good and the bad, we will find ourselves in a better headspace in spite of what we are dealing with at the moment.

That is what this 31-day devotion and journal, *Thirty-One Reasons to Praise,* is here to help you do. I want to assist you in finding praise in your pain, recognizing the good in the glum moments, finding peace in the midst of your process, and maintaining joy on this Jesus journey.

Here is how it works:

Each day includes:

Daily Scriptures

The main Scripture appears at the top of your devotion introducing the topic of the day. At the end of your devotion is a list of other Scriptures included in the passage for additional study.

Make sure to spend time throughout the day meditating on these words as God leads (Psalm 1:2-3).

All Scriptures are from the New King James Version (NKJV) unless otherwise stated.

31 Devotions

The devotion is the primary subject matter for the day. They are written to inspire you and get you thinking about why you can praise God in the midst of things that might not feel praiseworthy.

Although *Thirty-One Reasons to Praise* is designed to be read one devotion per day to give you time to meditate and apply what you have learned, that may not be your style. You can read this book in whatever way gives you the greatest sense of help.

A Prayer of Thanksgiving/Praise

At the end of each devotion, you are encouraged to pray and praise.

Prayers of thanksgiving are used to speak God's word into our lives. Read them to yourself or read them aloud. Not only does speaking and hearing the word increase our faith, but God hears the prayers of His children and is willing to respond to us (Romans: 10:17, John 14:14).

One thing I love about the Bible is that when we utilize it, it works. Speaking the word over your life with praise on your lips will have wonderfully positive effects on your mental, emotional, and physical world. I cannot wait for you to see the manifestation.

Journal Application

Journaling can be a helpful tool in solidifying what you have read or learned. Application is the whole point of these sections so the word comes alive for you. It can be a freeing experience. I pray God will speak to you throughout the entire devotion but especially during your journaling time.

I pray you are encouraged and find at least one more reason to praise God.

It's time to experience the peace associated with our praise. I know I am ready, are you?

Let's get started!

Day One

He Understands...

Great is our Lord, and mighty in power; His understanding is infinite.

-Psalm 147:5

One morning I got off the phone with a close friend and broke down in tears. I asked myself a super serious question, "Why in the world are you crying?"

The answer came quickly, "I just wished they understood me. They think they understand, but they don't know. They don't know. Why don't they get me right now?"

The day before this mini-breakdown I read Psalm 147 and verse 5 came flooding back to my remembrance! It was like hearing God say, "It's ok because I understand you!"

The Scripture says that His understanding (insight, wisdom, capacity to know how to move forward with you) is infinite (so great we can't even put a number or measurement on it).[1]

I know that sometimes we want the people we love, work for, work with, interact with to get everything about us and be able to deal with and understand every emotional high, middle, and low but that is an unfair expectation to put on them. We can barely understand ourselves sometimes! I know we want them to understand the unspoken things in our lives. I know we want them to understand why their actions frustrate us or why their inaction brings us a sense of sadness, but the reality is the only one who knows every intimate detail of our lives and can comprehend exactly what we are going through without us saying a word is God

Himself. The only one who can accurately assess our thoughts, desires, and situations is God. This is a good thing to know!

We've been looking for someone to understand us and here we have Scripture that validates there is one who always has and always will! He created us perfectly in His image and has the deepest understanding of us that no man or woman here on this earth can match.

Imagine someone understanding every detail about you and your life and choosing to love you and stick with you every moment of every day. That is who God is to you!

So praise Him for His knowledge of you. Praise Him for being a God that can count every single hair on your head. Praise Him for being a God that understands exactly what you are going through and feels your pain but also sees far into the future knowing what you will gain from this moment. Praise Him for understanding you and how the things around you work so that He can place you in perfect position to receive more of Him!

You definitely have a reason to praise!

Scriptures: Psalm 147:5; Matthew 10:30 MSG; Hebrews 4:15; Romans 8:28

Prayer of Praise: God I thank you for having an infinite understanding of all the things that are going on within me and around me! Thank you for knowing the deepest desires of my soul. I thank you that when I don't get it or don't know what to do that I can lean on your understanding and be led by your Holy Spirit! Thank you, God! Thank you, God, for giving me yet another reason to praise! In Jesus' name, amen.

What does Psalm 147:5 mean to you?

_____

_____

_____

_____

_____

_____

Is there anyone in your life that you wished would have a deeper understanding of you and what you may be facing in your life?

_____

How does today's devotion cause you to look at this person and situation now?

_____

_____

_____

_____

What else is on your mind? Let God know:

_____

_____

_____

_____

_____

_____

_____

_____

Day Two

He Provides Peace

You will keep him in perfect peace, whose mind is stayed on You, because he trusts in You.

-Isaiah 26:3

So many of us lack peace as we go through our days but in this Scripture, we have a promise that we can cash in our sorrows, frustrations, anxiety, anger, or any other negative feeling for peace anytime we are in need.

To redeem this gift of peace, there is something we have to do. We have to shift our hearts, thoughts, wants, and needs over to God.

Whatever it is that has caused you to feel a lack of peace is not bigger than God. Instead of dwelling on what you feel you lack, you must praise God for what you know is already yours in the spirit. Peace!

Philippians 4:7 tells us we can receive the peace that surpasses all understanding, peace that guards our hearts and minds. This gift is a big deal. The guarding of our hearts can direct us into more positive places both mentally and physically.

If you feel that you lack peace, God has given us a list of things we can meditate on to *feel* the God of peace in our lives. Just look at Philippians 4:8. It tells us to think on things that are noble, just, pure, lovely, things of good report, and things that are praiseworthy. These thoughts will help you activate this blessing in your life.

So right now, at this moment, that's what you have to do. It's okay to thank Him for the peace that is already yours even if it doesn't *feel* like you have it. Allow your praise to take you to a place of relief.

Scriptures: Isaiah 26:3; Philippians 4:6-8; Proverbs 4:23

Prayer of Praise: God I thank you for peace that surpasses all understanding. I thank you that if I continue to magnify who you are in my life that I can receive this gift of peace in full. I thank you that there is NOTHING on this earth that is bigger than you so I will no longer magnify the negative! I thank you that there are noble, just, pure, lovely, and praiseworthy things to think about! Bring them to my awareness even now. This promise that you will keep me in perfect peace if my mind stays on you is one. Thank you, God! Thank you, God, for giving me yet another reason to praise! In Jesus' name, amen.

Read Psalm 34:14 and fill in the blanks:

Seek _peace_ and _pursue it_.

How can you do these two things today?

Focusing on God and His goodness
Changing my thinking.
Choosing to be positive

Sometimes it helps to have positive thoughts in mind in case negative thoughts show up. Read Philippians 4:8, choose which positive thoughts you will focus on today, and then get specific.

Example:
Praiseworthy thought: I will praise God for my ability to control my thoughts.

I will praise God for His promises of peace

If you feel your peace slipping, come back to this list and think about these things. Be intentional in pursuing your peace today!

Day Three

I Have ALL the Spiritual Blessings

All praise to God, the Father of our Lord Jesus Christ, who has blessed us with every spiritual blessing in the heavenly realms because we are united with Christ.

-Ephesians 1:3 NLT

I woke up one morning in need. I allowed the actions of others and even the negative thoughts I had about myself to consume me, and I labeled myself unworthy. Unworthy of love, unworthy of time, unworthy of the call of God on my life, unworthy of the gifts I've been blessed with, unworthy of the people around me, just plain unworthy.

That particular morning I needed to *understand* that I was worthy. I *know* what the Scriptures say. But I needed my head knowledge to encourage my heart so that in that weak moment I would actually *believe* it. I needed to know without a shadow of a doubt that I was worth it in every area of my life.

I found my way to Ephesians 1 and verse 3 where three words stuck out to me, *every spiritual blessing*. As I studied this passage, I realized that every single spiritual blessing; Ok wait, let me say it one more time a little differently, **ALL** the spiritual blessings there are to have are mine. Mine! And here's the kicker, I didn't have to do anything to get them. They are mine because I'm united with Christ. And all these blessings are yours because you're united with Him.

You might be wondering, what are the spiritual blessings? I thought the same thing. They are listed throughout the word of God, but we can see many of them right here in the following verses.

First, let's make a distinction between spiritual blessings and temporal blessings. Essentially, spiritual blessings are obtained through our faith in God. They are promises that come from Heaven, and we have eternal access to them, meaning they last forever.

Temporal blessings, on the other hand, are not guaranteed, and if we do obtain them, they are not guaranteed to last forever. This point is obvious when we look at the disparity between what some families or individuals have and what others don't. Many temporal blessings can be manifested physically, and they are subject to change. Again, none of these temporal blessings are guaranteed to us at all times, not even our health.

The reality is there are times we get sick and have to call on God for healing. Then there are times where our bodies and minds are performing optimally. Some have good health their whole life while some suffer from chronic illnesses. Some have more money than the law should allow while others never see $10 in their bank account at a time. While we won't get into a debate about why God allows certain things I believe we all have a reason to praise Him in spite of what we may be lacking in temporal blessings.

Ephesians 1:3-14 promises us **ALL** spiritual blessings. It doesn't matter who we are or where we come from; we can have every good thing God has promised us from Heaven. That, my friend is what caused me to feel worthy!

If you read verses 3-14 in whatever version floats your boat towards understanding, we see that some of these spiritual blessings include:

- Being loved by God
- Being chosen by God
- Being seen without fault by God
- Being a part of God's family which gives Him great pleasure
- An outpouring of His kindness and grace

- Freedom purchased by the blood so that we're forgiven
- An outpouring of His wisdom and understanding

When I recognized what God gave me access to, I couldn't help but feel worthy. If God felt that way about me and entrusted all these things to me, then what does it matter what others felt or even what I felt? I had to realign my thoughts with God's and so, I praised.

I thanked Him for all the things I listed above and then I spoke them over myself. It warmed my heart and spirit, and I found my worth in Him. The only consistent, constant, unchanging being in my life. And the only one in yours. So praise Him that EVERY spiritual blessing is already yours!

Scriptures: Ephesians 1:3-14

Prayer of Praise: God I thank you for loving me and for choosing me in spite of everything you knew I could and would do wrong. Thank you for seeing me without fault and wanting me to be a part of your family. Thank you for deeming me worthy enough to pour out your kindness, grace, wisdom, and understanding into my life and thank you for the freedom and forgiveness you have granted me through your Son. God, I thank you that ALL these spiritual blessings and more are mine, and I thank you that no matter how I feel, I am worthy to receive them. Thank you, God! Thank you, God, for giving me yet another reason to praise! In Jesus' name, amen.

Read Ephesians 1:3-14.

What do the spiritual blessings in verses 3-14 mean to you?

_____

_____

_____

_____

_____

_____

_____

_____

Write down the blessings that speak to your heart most today and state the reason why.

Loved by God
Being seen without fault
Being chosen by God
His kindness and grace

_____

_____

_____

_____

_____

As often as you can, remind yourself of these spiritual blessings. Write them on a notecard, take this book with you, or simply memorize them.

You're worthy of every spiritual blessing listed solely based on you being united with Christ. What a blessing!

Day Four

He's Here, and He's Mine

Don't be afraid, for I am with you. Don't be discouraged, for I am your God. I will strengthen you and help you. I will hold you up with my victorious right hand.

-Isaiah 41:10 NLT

Life can be rough, it can be tough, it can discouraging, it can feel lonely, it can feel like it is beating you upside the head with a wooden plank, but this is where praise comes in. This is when we shift our focus to our mighty and matchless Creator and remember the words that He has promised us here in the Scripture.

We have a reason to praise God because we don't have to be afraid or worried. He promises us that He will never leave us or abandon us. He is with us in everything we are going through. When it feels like we are alone He wants you to remember that you are never alone in the Spirit.

While there are times we want to find this assurance in the people around us, God is the only one that can be with us 24/7. Take pleasure in that! Take pleasure that when you go into the testing facility, He can come. When you go into surgery, He can be there too. When you are broken on the inside crying into your pillow in the middle of the night, He is there with you.

If you are feeling discouraged, it's the perfect time to praise because He is saying, "look I am your God!" That is exciting because there are definitely perks to being one of the loves of His life. He promises to strengthen and help us and then He gets really deep and lets us know that He is holding us up with His victorious hand. We don't have to worry about feeling weak because we are made strong in Him. We don't have to worry when people aren't carrying through on their end of the bargain or helping us in our weak moments, even if we were there for them in theirs because HE is available and willing to help us.

You don't have to be discouraged because it *looks* like you're losing. He will hold you up with His victorious right hand! You are winning just by knowing and receiving Him. Let Him be what He promised to be to you. Let Him carry it out. Praise Him now giving Him access to take away every negative feeling you may have had before reading this passage.

Scriptures: Isaiah 41:10; Deuteronomy 31:6

Prayer of Praise: God I thank you that when I feel afraid, discouraged, or weak you have made beautiful promises to me that I know you intend to keep. Thank you for being with me and never leaving me! Thank you that even when it's quiet, I know you haven't forsaken me. Thank you for being my God and choosing to be my God in spite of it all. Thank you for strengthening me in my heart, mind, body, and spirit. Thank you for holding me up with your victorious right hand proving to me and anyone else who needs to see that I will always win with you! Thank you, God! Thank you, God, for giving me yet another reason to praise! In Jesus' name, amen.

Where are you feeling discouraged in your life right now?

_____

_____

_____

_____

_____

Let's do something with what you just wrote. Today I want you to practice encouraging yourself in this area or these areas.

Fill in the blanks of the following affirmation...

I will not be afraid because God is with me. I will not be discouraged about _____ because He is my God. He will strengthen and help me even in this. He is holding me up with His victorious hand. Therefore, I am not alone. I am winning!

Now speak this truth aloud three times and praise Him for being there with you, even in this!

I will not be afraid because God is with me. I will not be discouraged about _____ because He is my God. He will strengthen and help me even in this. He is holding me up with His victorious hand. Therefore, I am not alone. I am winning!

Now speak this truth aloud three times and praise Him for being there with you, even in this!

Day Five

I Ain't Got No Worries

Therefore I say to you, do not worry about your life, what you will eat or what you will drink; nor about your body, what you will put on. Is not life more than food and the body more than clothing?

-Matthew 6:25

Even though the world might try to get us to believe that we have worries as the bill collectors call, the cupboards look bare, or our friends or family members are in the hospital, we should not worry about our life, what we will eat, or even what we are to put on.

In following verses, God clearly shows us that worrying is pointless because it doesn't add anything to our stature. Worry doesn't make us look better, it doesn't give us a sense of achievement, it doesn't cause us to glow with hope, and it doesn't bring peace. Matter of fact, it takes away. It causes us to lose faith and our trust that God will do the very thing He promised. Our praise should stem from the fact that even when we are given reasons to worry, we don't have to!

When I first saw this Scripture I only praised God because I knew He would provide with material things. But when I really read it and saw the word *life* I thought, "Man, that has everything to do with everything within me and around me. The spiritual and the natural. I really shouldn't be worried about anything because God has it handled."

If God can care for the birds of the air and lilies of the field, I'm confident that He will care and provide for His creations, His daughters and sons!

Child of God, you are covered, provided for, and taken care of. Even if you don't see it in the natural (happening right before you) trust that it has already been handled in the spirit. Please wait on the manifestation. God is a good God who keeps His promises. Trust that. He takes care of His creation because it pleases Him to do so. Rest in that.

Scriptures: Matthew 6:25-34; Numbers 23:19

Prayer of Praise: God I thank you for reminding me that when anxiety or depression hits, I don't have to worry about anything! I thank you that you are taking care of every single need for me, my family, and my friends simply because you promised that you would! I thank you for reminding me that I am not helping anyone or anything by worrying. I thank you for providing for me in the past, that you are currently providing for me, and that you will continue to do so even when it looks like I'm going without. Even when it looks like the world is falling apart...I trust you! Thank you, God! Thank you, God, for giving me yet another reason to praise! In Jesus' name, amen.

I've been worried about these things lately:

_____

_____

_____

_____

_____

_____

State this phrase:
I've just been reminded that none of these things are bigger than God! He wants me to rest assured that He is handling it. I trust that God is handling it!

Today, I pray that when the above worries attempt to infiltrate your peaceful moments that you will counter them with the word of truth.

Take the worries you listed above and fill them in the blanks provided below...

_____ is/are not bigger than God! He is already taking care of it! I have no reason to worry!

_____ is/are not bigger than God! He is already taking care of it! I have no reason to worry!

_____ is/are not bigger than God! He is already taking care of it! I have no reason to worry!

Speaking life over your situation will do wonders!

Day Six

He Won't Lie to Me

God is not a man, that He should lie, Nor a son of man, that He should repent. Has He said, and will He not do? Or has He spoken, and will He not make it good?

- Numbers 23:19

People lie. We've lied, and we've been lied to. Because of this, it can be a little difficult to place our trust or confidence in others or even in ourselves. But here is one reason to praise, although we are made in His image, God is nothing like us.

What do I mean? He is perfect, He is blameless, and the love He has for us is unconditional. God made us a promise that He will not lie to us and because of His character, He can't go back on that. So even if you feel like you can't trust the people in your house, on your job, at your church, in the grocery store, or even yourself, praise God that there is one that you can fully trust in all things. Him!

If He told you that you're healed, believe Him. If He told you, you can have that family, believe Him. If He told you those family members and friends are going to get saved, believe Him. If He told you He is going to use you to change the world, believe Him. If He told you not to worry about those false allegations that have been brought against you, believe Him. Shoot, if He told you not to worry about the true allegations that have been brought against you, believe Him.

Trust Him! He is not like us. He isn't fickle. He won't go back on His word. He makes good on every promise. Sometimes our narrow-minded ways of thinking cause us to miss out on the promises of God and make us believe He lied. Not true! Take Him out of the box and be open to Him coming through in ways you could have never thought or imagined.

Scriptures: Numbers 23:19; Genesis 1:27; Psalm 18:30; Romans 8:38-39

Prayer of Praise: God I thank you that I can trust you fully! I thank you that when you make a promise, you keep it! I thank you that you have given me the strength to do that same thing. I believe you will do what you said, God. I thank you for being honest with me even when it hurts. I thank you for being a place of safety and trust. Thank you, God! Thank you, God, for giving me yet another reason to praise! In Jesus' name, amen.

What are some things God has promised you? Write them here:

_____

_____

_____

_____

_____

_____

Do you need to know some of the promises God has made to you? Read Deuteronomy 28. This chapter shows us what our obedience opens us up to. Write down all of the promises you see or the ones that stand out to you.

_____

_____

_____

_____

_____

_____

_____

Now it's time to speak these promises over your life, so you gain confidence that they are for you!

God is not a man that He should lie. Therefore, He will allow for

_____

to take place simply because He said so. I'm grateful for the patience to see it come to fruition.

Keep speaking this over your life until you believe it, be grateful for the patience He can give you in the process, and praise God for it even before you see the manifestation!

Day Seven
I Have Permission to SLEEP

It is vain for you to rise up early, to sit up late, to eat the bread of sorrows; For so He gives His beloved sleep.

-Psalm 127:2 NKJV

It is useless for you to work so hard from early morning until late at night, anxiously working for food to eat; for God gives rest to his loved ones.

- Psalm 127:2 NLT

We live in a, 'I'll sleep when I'm dead' culture. We are busy, busy, busy all of the time. We watch people brag that they are a part of 'team no sleep' and that they never rest...Ever. They even pride themselves on being successful and rich regardless of the stress or strain it may cause on them or the people close to them. I'm tired just thinking about it.

Let me say this, I believe in the power of hard work, persistence, and even pulling all-nighters to finish a task but you will never hear me tell someone that I will sleep when I'm dead! What?! No! While I avoid sleep some days and it seems to escape me others, I love sleep far too much to wait until death to do it. I need it now!

The reality is, God desires for us to rest. He hasn't said work, work, work and never sleep or only take catnaps!

Lord, I'm preaching to myself right now.

He desires for us to sleep. Today I just want you to thank God that He has not taken sleep off the table. I want you to thank God that He desires for us to not only rest in Him spiritually but for us to close our eyes and allow for Him to rejuvenate our bodies while we do.

The Scripture says that He gives His beloved sleep! In the New International Version, it says, *For He grants sleep to those He loves*. How sweet is that?

Look, if you're a child of God you have a promise of sleep. You don't have to wait until you die. There is no point in staying up all day and all night working to provide when we know good and well God said don't worry about all that (Matthew 6:25-34).

Someone might be saying, "But I don't seem to get any sleep, does this mean God doesn't love me?" No, that doesn't mean that at all. That could be for a number of reasons. Maybe you haven't cast your cares on God, so your worry is keeping you up. Maybe your work has become an idol, and you'll have to go to God and ask Him how to replace it with Him once again. Maybe God is calling you to a deeper level of intimacy with Him and just desires a conversation before allowing you to fall asleep. Maybe you need to be praying or reading your word. Maybe it's something biological that seeing a doctor can help you pinpoint. Only you know.

Here is what I do know, God loves us, and since we know this to be true (just look at what He did for us on the cross) then this promise of sweet, sweet sleep is ours. We don't have to wait until death. We can do it now! I mean, only if you are in a safe place where sleep is acceptable. Do not fall asleep at your job right now. No. Don't do it. But expect to get some rest tonight. Take a break from all the work for just eight hours. It will be there tomorrow. And my prayer is that God will give you rest. This is a reason to praise!

Scriptures: Psalm 127:2 (read as many versions as you can of this verse); Matthew 11:28; Matthew 6:25-34

Prayer of Praise: Lord, how I thank you for giving me a solid reason to go to bed tonight without having to worry about provision. I thank you that you are giving me permission to not bring all of my work home every night but to take the time to steal away and sleep! I thank you that although it's popular in our culture to work, work, work until your body shuts you down that I have permission to work, rest, and sleep. Thank you for loving me so much that you have incorporated this into my life! I pray that I will be able to rest and trust in you so that I can experience the sweet and beautiful gift of peace and rest you've given me. Thank you, God! Thank you, God, for giving me yet another reason to praise! In Jesus' name, amen.

Write the reasons you haven't been sleeping or resting at night down. What is keeping you up and why?

_____

_____

_____

_____

_____

_____

_____

_____

Read 1 Peter 5:7.

Take this time to cast your cares on God. You can write them out and throw them into the air or into a trashcan. Or you can just read what you listed on your paper and say, "Lord, I give these to you right now."

_____

_____

_____

_____

_____

_____

_____

_____

_____

_____

If *it* can wait, please wait until you have had enough sleep to positively and effectively deal with the situation.

Day Eight
He Heals the Brokenhearted

He heals the brokenhearted and binds up their wounds.

-Psalm 147:3

I think it's pretty safe to say that most of us have experienced heartbreak in our lifetime. It can be a debilitating feeling. Heartbreak has led even the most pristine, saved, accomplished, wealthy, joy-filled people into addiction, depression, anxiety, isolation, and even suicidal thoughts and attempts.

It can literally feel like death is upon you and that you will not be able to get past the hurt of that moment. Oh, but God has made us a promise. A promise for all those who have, are, or going to suffer from heartbreak in their lives. He says that, *He heals the brokenhearted and binds up their wounds*!

Someone might be thinking, "Then where is He? My heart is breaking, and I feel like I'm going to lose it." The answer, He's right there. He promised He would never leave you nor forsake you! In Psalm 34:18 it says that, *The Lord is near to those who have a broken heart*. He is right there! But here's the catch...you have to reach out to Him.

He hates it when we hurt. Think about how we feel when someone or something has caused someone we love and care about to feel broken. You want to fix it. You might even want to exchange places with them. Well God, He wants to fix it. He wants to exchange your cares with His love, but you have to reach out.

I've spent most of my adult life trying to fill the holes of my brokenness and brokenhearted moments by mistakenly placing people, places, and things in His position. It was quick and easy to take a few shots of tequila and get into a good place for the moment. It was more convenient to rest in the arms of someone who only *said* they loved me. It was more comforting to run to friends and cry because they could give me immediate advice.

But the liquor couldn't talk back and made me feel horrible the next day. The arms and ears of the ones I confided in could only be there for so long, and they could only give me advice based on their limited knowledge of the situation, the word, their experience, and most of all their limited knowledge of me. But God's wisdom is infinite. He knows everything about us and how to navigate us to a place of healing in Him. If we lay it all at His feet and allow for Him to be the remedy, we will experience the healing. If we allow Him to bind up every wound, we will not have to worry about the wound reopening with every little trigger.

This means taking every emotion you feel and searching the Scriptures to see what they say about them. It means praying to God about the situation and listening for a response. It also means taking these promises of God and praising Him that each and every one of them applies to you. Even the one we find in Psalm 147:3. He can heal your broken heart. Take time with God daily (and each moment that feels unbearable) and receive your healing. He's there. He's waiting. Find rest in His love. Find healing for your heart, mind, and soul. This is definitely a reason to praise!

Scriptures: Psalm 147:3; Psalm 34:18; Deuteronomy 31:6; Hebrews 13:5; 1 Peter 5:7; Psalm 55:22; Psalm 147:5

Prayer of Praise: God I thank you that even though I have tried many things, none of them can promise to heal the brokenness of my heart and actually fulfill that promise. I thank you that you can heal the hurt of yesterday, today, and even the heartbreak that may occur in my tomorrow. Thank you, Lord, for loving my heart so much that you would stand near me until I recognize that I need to reach out. Thank you for being there and ready to bandage me up so that I can learn to fully receive your love and walk in that same love. God, I want to be healed! And I thank you that it's a promise that's already done in my life. I believe it now! I receive it now! In Jesus' name! Thank you, God! Thank you, God, for giving me yet another reason to praise! Amen.

What is currently breaking your heart?

_____

_____

_____

_____

_____

_____

_____

Write down the promise we find in Psalm 147:3.

_____

_____

Do you trust this promise is for you in this situation and why?

_____

_____

_____

_____

How can you reach out to God regarding this today?

_____

_____

_____

_____

_____

_____

Sometimes healing takes time. When you cry out, God hears and has a plan in action to rescue you just as He did with the people of God in Exodus (Exodus 2:24-25). Hold tight! Your help is here!

Day Nine
I Matter

But now indeed there are many members, yet one body. And the eye cannot say to the hand, "I have no need of you"; nor again the head to the feet, "I have no need of you." No, much rather, those members of the body which seem to be weaker are necessary.

-1 Corinthians 12:20-22

What a blessing! We matter. We all matter. All of our gifts matter. We are needed even if we *feel* we are the weakest link. We all serve a heavy purpose in the body of Christ.

It's crazy how divided people can become over gifts and talents. It's crazy how we can beat ourselves up because our gifts and talents don't look like the person who is getting all the attention and accolades. We begin to compare ourselves to one another and before you know it we are coveting someone else's gifts, position, status, lifestyle, and lives. But God tells us that we are **all** necessary. Whether you feel you are the weakest person in the room or not you are needed!

I love how the New Living Translation puts it. It says, ***In fact, some parts of the body that seem weakest and least important are the most necessary.*** Stop counting yourself out! This translation uses the word *seem*, meaning something that appears to be true, something that is probable. It doesn't mean it is so.

You, child of God, are fearfully and wonderfully made by God. He has placed gifts inside of you that are innate to you. God doesn't give us our gifts just to give them. He doesn't place things inside of us that don't matter. He doesn't waste space or time. You matter! You are not wasted space! That is a major reason to praise Him.

Even if people have counted you out, even if YOU have counted yourself out, the word of God tells us that YOU are most necessary. This kingdom can't move forward the way it needs to without you. There are people in your life that need you in position so they can fully operate in theirs. You matter!

Praise God because you matter! Not because anyone else says that you do, not because I say that you do, but because God says that you do. Read verse 22 again.

You are necessary!

Think about it; there is no way that people could run multibillion-dollar corporations without even the lowest paid employee. When one service is provided, it affects every other branch of the organization.

I was chatting with the youth in my church about the actors and actresses we see on television. I asked them who were the most important people on these shows and movies. Most, of course, said, "The actors." We had to dig a little deeper to see that without the people who film the shows, provide the lighting, provide the sound and set up the equipment, the producers, directors, casting directors, writers, editors, property masters, assistants, and security, we wouldn't get to see characters come to life on our TV screens daily. Everyone is important.

We are not supposed to live life as if we are a one-man show. It's not possible. No matter what we have learned growing up, we cannot do things alone. We need each other, and nobody is better than the next. We should be acting with love towards one another because well, we all matter.

You may think your gifts don't matter, but they do. You may think your gifts aren't recognized, but they are. God sees and is aware of every great thing that resides on the inside of you. And honestly, God's view of you is the only one that matters. Praise God for that.

Now go out and be fully you and walk in your gifts praising Him all along the way simply because you matter to Him and the kingdom.

Scriptures: 1 Corinthians 12:20-22; Psalm 139:14

Prayer of Praise: Lord, I thank you that I matter. No matter what anyone has said or what anyone says about me I believe your word. I am necessary to the kingdom, and I can make a great impact simply because I've been fearfully and wonderfully made by a God that placed gifts on the inside of me. Thank you for helping me cultivate my gifts, thank you for showing me my gifts, (thank you in advance for showing me my gifts) and thank you for letting me know I matter to you. Thank you, God! Thank you, God, for giving me yet another reason to praise! In Jesus' name, amen.

One major concern many people have is not knowing their gifts.

We as a culture tend to magnify certain talents and minimize others, so some people who aren't artistic, athletic, or entertainers feel left out in the gift department. Even in the church!

Hey child of purpose, don't limit our God!

Your gifts are there. Do you know them? If you don't that's ok, here is some help.

Ask yourself, "What am I able to do fairly easy that takes others a bit more time?" Or, "What do I do well? No matter how many times I turn away from it, I always find myself right back here..."
(It could be crunching numbers, cooking, deescalating intense situations, reading and understanding instructions, getting kids to stay quiet, getting people excited about boring things, writing, learning, teaching, speaking, understanding what people are going through, etc.)

Please do not limit yourself or exclude the things you think do not make money or things you've seen others do "better." That's not what this is about.

Now, list these things below and praise God for every one. Add to the list as they come up. You matter! And the kingdom of God is in need of your gifts and the way you use them.

_____

_____

_____

_____

_____

_____

_____

_____

Ask someone you trust what they identify as your areas of talent. When you get some feedback, write them here even if you don't agree. (*Sometimes others see more in us than we see in ourselves*)

_____

_____

_____

_____

Prayer: Lord, help me to learn more about my gifts and to exercise them so I can become stronger and more confident in them. Thank you for blessing me with them. I pray I use them for your glory, in Jesus' name, amen.

Do you feel like you matter to the kingdom or to the people around you? Use this space to talk to God about it.

_____

_____

_____

_____

_____

_____

_____

_____

_____

_____

_____

_____

_____

_____

_____

Day Ten

There Are Good Days and There Are Bad Days
I Can Praise Him on Both

In everything give thanks; for this is the will of God in Christ Jesus for you.

- 1 Thessalonians 5:18

Every day won't be perfect. If we are honest, some days can just plain suck! But the reality is, not every day is bad and if we have the right perspective even the worst day of our year can be seen in a positive light.

Think back to one of the best days of your life. Something super awesome might have happened, or it could have been real laid back with you hanging out in front of a TV all day getting to take naps and rest. Either way, I want you to recall that day. Remember the sense of relief you felt, the happiness or the laughter you experienced, or the calm you felt getting to hang out with people that genuinely care about you.

Do you have it?

Have you pictured it? Don't worry we have time.

Got it?

Okay, awesome! Now understand this, the same peace, relief, and joy that we feel on our good days, is the same peace, relief, and joy we can feel on our most difficult days.

I'm not saying you won't have moments of sadness, heaviness, anger, or even tears, but I am saying that if we focus our eyes on God and thank Him for being Him we can activate the spiritual blessings of peace, joy, strength, and endurance that God gives us through the Holy Spirit right then and there.

The Holy Spirit is awesome because He is on call 24 hours a day seven days a week. The emergency pager is always available for you to call every single moment of your life.

If you are having a bad day today, you can praise Him because you're able to access the spiritual blessing of joy! Even though tears may be falling there can still be a sense of peace that tells you, you're going to be okay.

You're going to be okay!

The word of God says we should bless the Lord at all times! That we should rejoice always, pray without ceasing, and in everything give thanks! And it's important that we do. Even if today isn't the best day of your life praise Him for the good days. Praise Him for the times that have been completely awesome and the days that haven't been so great because you're still here. He is keeping you. Peace, joy, strength and endurance are still yours for the taking, for the having, for the keeping.

Even though every day might not be good, God *is* good every day. Rest on that. Praise Him for the fact you are alive. Praise Him because He is good and that no matter what you're dealing with He can turn your day from blah to awesome right now!

We *definitely* have a reason to praise Him!

Scriptures: 1 Thessalonians 5:16-18; Psalm 34:1; Isaiah 26:3; Romans 8:28

Prayer of Praise: God I thank you just because you're good! I thank you that no matter what I am going through your peace, joy, strength, and endurance is still mine for the taking and keeping. God, I thank you that you do not take my praise away just because it's a tough day. I thank you that I'm able to enter into a deeper level of your presence through praise at this moment. I thank you that there have been good days, and I thank you for the bad because I know you will work them out for the good! Thank you, God! Thank you, God, for giving me yet another reason to praise! In Jesus' name, amen.

Why do you think it's important to praise God, especially on bad days?

_____

_____

_____

_____

_____

What happens when you place a magnifying glass on an object?

_____

_____

_____

The same things happen when we magnify our problems. They appear bigger than what they really are! If we look to God and magnify Him, we will see Him larger than life and bigger than our circumstances!

What promises or characteristics of God will you choose to magnify today?

_____

_____

_____

_____

_____

_____

_____

Don't forget to come back to this list as often as you need to.

JOURNAL

Day Eleven

He Never Changes

Jesus Christ is the same yesterday, today, and forever.

-Hebrews 13:8

Your world could be flipped upside down right now. New people entering, people you thought were going to be there forever leaving, one job laying people off over here, this job moving everyone clear across the country over there. The Spirit of God may have you moving from one church to another, or you see divorce, break ups, death, and disease all around you. Man, it is exhausting!

When life is moving, when nothing in your view looks the same, God has still given us a reason to praise. He is the same yesterday, today, and forever. He makes promises and keeps them. He is consistent and faithful to His word. When there is absolutely no one else to lean on, God remains steady so you can put all your weight on Him. When there is no one else to talk to He says, "Cast your cares on me." When there is no peace, He says, "Keep your eyes on me, and I will give you perfect peace." When there is no one to watch your back, He has promised that He will never leave you or forsake you and that you can hide in the shadow of His wings.

He is the same even when we change, for better or for worse. He would be the same even if we walked away. He is the same even when we slide all the way back to where He brought us from the first three times. He is the same when people attempt to change the word to fit their way of living. He is the same when people ask, "Where is your God?" He is the same whether we believe that He is or not.

So here is the reason we have to praise Him, no matter what we are going through, no matter what generation we live in, we can trust that God is the same God now that He was when Moses was floating down the river as a baby. He is the same God that sent Jesus on a journey that put us in a faultless relationship with Him. He is the same God that pulled you out of the last mess you were in. He is the same God that will give you peace and joy in the midst of the storm. And guess what else? He will be the same God tomorrow when you need Him.

Praise Him for never changing!

Scriptures: Hebrews 13:8; Numbers 23:19; 1 Peter 5:7; Isaiah 26:3; Deuteronomy 31:6; Psalm 91:4

Prayer of Praise: God, I thank you for your consistency. I thank you that you're consistent even when I'm not! I thank you for being consistent even when the people in my life who promised to be, couldn't be any longer. I thank you for being a God that never changes making it easier to get to know you, understand you, and for me to trust in you. I thank you for loving me consistently. I thank you that your word will never change and neither will you. I thank you that you were the same yesterday, I thank you that you are the same right now, and I thank you that you will be the same God tomorrow. Thank you, God! Thank you, God, for giving me yet another reason to praise! In Jesus' name, amen.

Write out Hebrews 13:8.

_____

_____

_____

What does this verse mean to you right now at this very moment?
Tell God about it.

_____

_____

_____

_____

_____

_____

_____

_____

_____

_____

_____

_____

_____

_____

_____

_____

_____

_____

_____

_____

Day Twelve
Missed Opportunities Are Opportunities

No, dear brothers and sisters, I have not achieved it, but I focus on this one thing: Forgetting the past and looking forward to what lies ahead, I press on to reach the end of the race and receive the heavenly prize for which God, through Christ Jesus, is calling us.

-Philippians 3:13-14 NLT

We all have experienced missed opportunities. Whether they were big or small they had the potential to leave us feeling bummed. Maybe you missed an opportunity to praise God, share His goodness with someone, or stand firm on your convictions. Maybe you missed a deadline that was important to you, you didn't get a job you wanted, didn't get to go out on that date, or you missed the opportunity to get a deal that you were hoping for. Maybe you missed an opportunity for something I didn't list because man, we can miss so many things. Today I'm here to tell you that you can still praise God in this. Why? Because one, a missed opportunity doesn't mean that God is any less good and two, it gives God a chance to show you just how God He is!

When you miss out on an opportunity, you have to remember that it's not the end of the world. So you cannot dwell on it. You have to cast this care over to God and trust that if it's for you, you will get another shot. He will make a way for you to get another opportunity because when God begins a work, He finishes it.

God is a pro at bringing things He desires for us to pass because He knows at the end of the day it will bring Him glory and draw His children back to Him. God will give us opportunities to take make-up tests if we just so happened to drop the ball the first time around. He will give us chances to catch up if we just so happened not to be chosen by man for that last opportunity. It may look different the next time around, we may have to wait a little bit for it, and we may even incur an extra cost but if it's God and for us, we **will** get it. It's not a question. We should be able to praise God for this!

You have to let go of that moment of failure, that moment of disappointment, the feelings of shame, sadness, and discouragement and look forward to the opportunities that lie ahead. You have to forget about that moment because guess what? There is nothing you can do about it! However, you can be in control of your next steps (with God being your guide of course). You can walk in obedience to His directives and claim that thing that is for you. He might even show you that you didn't need that thing at all! **You won't know until you move forward**. You have to press towards the call, towards God, and as you do everything else will fall into place.

Again I say, it's not the end of the world when you miss out on something. It's okay to feel bummed out, but you cannot stay there! Drop it and don't allow it to negatively affect your day. Today has its own opportunities. Seize them! Don't miss them dwelling on what you've missed or lost. We must praise Him because we have an opportunity to grab what God has for us right now. In this moment. And like I mentioned above, if you are truly allowing yourself to be led by the Spirit of God then you might have an opportunity to reclaim the very thing you thought you lost. Trust Him!

Scriptures: Philippians 3:13-14 NLT; Philippians 1:6; 1 Peter 5:7; Proverbs 3:5-6; Revelation 3:7-8

Prayer of Praise: Lord it might be hard to say at times but I thank you for every missed opportunity. I thank you that those moments draw me closer to you, and I thank you that you respond. I'm so grateful that even in this, I can move forward and continue to press towards you. While I'm doing that, I know you will open doors that no man can shut. I trust you to lead me to the opportunities that are for me today, and I thank you that you are giving me an open heart to receive them in spite of what I lost yesterday. I love you and thank you that this missed opportunity can and will grow me in you. Thank you, God! Thank you, God, for giving me yet another reason to praise! In Jesus' name, Amen.

Missed opportunities can cause us to feel down, but that doesn't mean we can sit still and sulk forever.

Below, I want you to list some of your missed opportunities in the left-hand column.

Now on the right, write how can you press forward in spite of how you feel while preparing yourself to be ready when the next opportunity comes around.

MISSED OPPORTUNITIES	HOW WILL I PRESS FORWARD THE NEXT TIME?
Example: Failed my promotion test	Tears are fine, but I will study harder. I will take a course if they have one, I will apply to take the test again...I will obliterate the test this time and I will remind myself that I'm not a failure!

Day Thirteen
He Desires to Restore

I'll make up for the years of the locust, the great locust devastation—Locust savage, locust deadly, fierce locusts, locust of doom, that great locust invasion I sent your way. You'll eat your fill of good food. You'll be full of praises to your God, the God who has set you back on your heels in wonder. Never again will my people be despised. You'll know without question that I'm in the thick of your life with Israel, that I'm your God, yes, your God, the one and only real God. Never again will my people be despised.

-Joel 2:25-27 MSG

Loss can run you down to your lowest point. No matter what it is, if it was of great significance to you and you lose it, it can feel downright horrible. It may cause you to feel ashamed, angry, hurt, or confused. To be fair to both sides, some people are relieved for the loss they incur. But for those of you that are finding it difficult to deal with, you can praise God for one thing for sure, He can and will restore. He desires to put you back in a good place with Him. But He can only do that if you let Him.

If you don't believe that God can bring you back into a place of restoration (mentally, emotionally, spiritually, or physically) then you will block every spiritual and temporal blessing that He sends your way. Let me tell you how. You will literally reject the blessings by saying things like, "No, I'm not good enough" or "No, I messed that up the last time."

We don't want to stand in the way of what God is doing. It takes knowing the word to know that He will do what He said. He will make up for the years. So it doesn't matter if this was something that happened when you were three or something that happened an hour ago, God has a way of making up the time like you never lost it. His timing is different than ours and unlike us, He takes into account the entire picture.

Notice the Scripture says, the invasion that He sent their way. This might cause you to say, "Why would God send an invasion my way?" Well, first He's Sovereign. We may never fully understand why God does what He does, but we can trust that He knows what He's doing and will work everything out for the good of those who love Him, which we all do, and those who are called according to His purpose. We've accepted the call of faith to be in a relationship with Him, so we're good. But other than His Sovereignty sometimes God needs to allow a little bit of rain to happen to get our attention, to grow us, to strengthen us in areas we didn't know we were weak, or to call our attention to the true desires of our hearts. But after you have suffered a little while and have come to Him He promises some things. You will eat your fill of good food, you will be full of praise (and you know how praise can change our lives), you will be placed back on your heels (how great it feels to be back on your feet after feeling knocked down), and you will have a greater intimacy and knowledge of this God we love and serve!

To top it off, people are going to notice, and it will draw them to Christ as well. Every loss is an opportunity for you and someone who is watching you, to grow in God. Let that be a reason to praise as well.

Open your heart and get ready for the restoration. Expect it. Expect Him. He will make up for those years. Praise Him for that.

Scriptures: Joel 2:25-27; 2 Peter 3:8; Romans 8:28; 1 Peter 5:10

Prayer of Praise: It is a blessing to know that you are a God that restores. No matter what I feel I have lost, I can trust you to fill me with good things once again. I can trust that you will set me back on my feet and that my praise will be strengthened once again. I can trust that I won't be despised and that I will know, and others will too, that you are the one and true living God. I thank you that my testimony of loss can lead me to great gains and bring others into a knowledge of you. Thank you, God, for restoration in spite of what I may have done wrong or what I've done right! I open my heart, mind, spirit, body, and life to receive it now in Jesus' name. Thank you, God! Thank you, God, for giving me yet another reason to praise! Amen.

Are there any parts of this Scripture that are hard to deal with? Tell God about it. He appreciates honesty.

_____

_____

_____

_____

_____

_____

_____

_____

_____

_____

God will give you revelation regarding your concerns at the appropriate time. If He already has, record it here:

_____

_____

_____

_____

_____

_____

Are there any parts of the Scripture that give you hope? Tell God, and He'll be happy to show you how your hope and faith can make the manifestation in your life that much sweeter.

_____

_____

_____

_____

Remember, God will restore us to where we need to be. He won't place us back in dangerous situations or where we won't grow. He won't restore what will hurt us. Don't confuse His love of keeping you out of harms way with unfulfilled promise. Instead, be excited that what you get in your restoration season is exactly what you need.

What do you desire to see restored in your life?

_____

_____

_____

_____

_____

_____

_____

_____

_____

_____

_____

_____

_____

_____

_____

_____

_____

_____

_____

_____

_____

_____

Day Fourteen
His Hopes Are Greater Even When Life Hurts

For I know the thoughts that I think toward you, says the Lord, thoughts of peace and not of evil, to give you a future and a hope. Then you will call upon Me and go and pray to Me, and I will listen to you. And you will seek Me and find Me, when you search for Me with all your heart.

- Jeremiah 29:11-13

Even when it hurts there is a greater plan. I don't care what you are going through, I don't care what people are saying about you or what you are saying about you, there is a God that has peaceful and positive thoughts about you running through His mind all day. He loves you, He cherishes His relationship with you, and most of all He wants to prosper you in Him.

Even if your thoughts are a reason you have fallen into a dark space or your disobedience led to physical or mental bondage and hurt, you can rest assured there is a promise of peace and hope for you as well.

Everything that happens to us is a part of a greater story, a story that builds strength in us. A story that inspires others to find the strength they need to move forward. God will use everything we go through not only to encourage us and take us further but to assist in saving other's lives.

God can use your greatest hurt to do His greatest works. Stop feeling like you're being punished, stop thinking that God hates you, stop thinking that you aren't and can't be loved by God. This Scripture promises you that He thinks good things about you and wants good things for you. Open your heart and mind to receive His unfailing love.

Do yourself a favor, call on Him, pray (communicate) with Him, and trust that He is listening to everything you say. He will provide an answer. He will respond to your prayers. He promises that. Trust Him. Go to Him. Release your pain into His hands and remember what He said.

Scriptures: Jeremiah 29:11-13; Romans 8:28; Genesis 50:20; John 14:14

Prayer of Praise: I thank you that I can call on you, and you will incline your ear to me. I thank you that you, the creator of the universe and my soul, would take the time to listen to the petitions of my heart and that you will respond in a way that's best for my future and where you're taking me. Although I may long for the things that I miss in the flesh and the things that I lost that caused me hurt, I thank you for being here to comfort my spirit. I thank you for thinking peace filled thoughts about me, and I thank you that you have already planned a great future for me. I receive it in Jesus' name. Thank you, God! Thank you, God, for giving me yet another reason to praise! Amen.

Write out Jeremiah 29:11-13.

_____

_____

_____

_____

_____

_____

_____

What does this Scripture say to you right now? Spend a little time with God and share your thoughts. Release it all to Him.

_____

_____

_____

_____

_____

_____

_____

_____

_____

_____

_____

_____

_____

_____

_____

_____

_____

_____

Day Fifteen

He Will Strengthen My Heart

I would have lost heart, unless I had believed that I would see the goodness of the Lord in the land of the living. Wait on the Lord; be of good courage, and He shall strengthen your heart; Wait, I say, on the Lord!

-Psalm 27:13-14

I know the situation may hurt, or you may feel that you are at your wits end, it may feel that there is nothing left to give, and God is not hearing nor answering your prayers, but do not lose heart! This God, who promises never to leave us or forsake us, is there for you, inclining His ear to you because He has heard your cry. He is saying, do not lose heart, do not grow weary in well doing.

Our hearts need to be strengthened in God alone so that we don't go back to the things that may have caused us to get weak; So that we don't even have a desire or longing to go back to the things that caused us to want to fall apart.

You have to believe that you will see the goodness of the Lord, child of God. Not just after death but while you are alive here on this earth. You don't have to wait to experience God's goodness. It is all around you, and it even dwells inside of you. Remember that ALL spiritual blessings are for you.

There are two things this Scripture tells us we have to do.

1) Wait on God

Wait simply means to hope in, expect, be strong in,

Hope on God. Expect Him to come through for you! Yes, things might always *seem* to fail and work in everyone else's favor but yours, but that is no reason to stop expecting from a God that promises He will give you a future and hope. He *knows* what is best for you and is *willing* to give you the best. It may not come in the timing you desire, but it will come at the perfect time. I wish we had a sense of perfect timing, but the truth is we don't. Trust in the God that does.

What are some things you are expecting from God? Praise Him for them. There is nothing wrong with praising Him in advance for what you know He will do. It's telling God that you have complete and total confidence in Him and are not going to worry about a thing.

2) Be of good courage

He has not left you or abandoned you, and you will reap the benefits of your wait and what you have sown if you don't give up. If you don't lose heart. To not lose heart you have to believe that you can see God's goodness today while keeping a positive outlook on life. This brings strength, growth, and a magnitude of favor you couldn't even begin to imagine. He'll start doing exceedingly abundantly above all that you could ask or think. Praise Him for that.

The Scripture tells us to wait twice, so we know He means business. Rest in Him and, in the meantime, serve God as if all your prayers have already manifested in front of you. Serve Him, praise Him, and watch the way He moves in your life and the lives of others. Don't lose heart! Don't give up! Be encouraged child of God.

Stand firm on Him and praise Him in advance so that you don't miss your due season.

Scriptures: Psalm 27:13-14; Deuteronomy 31:6; Psalm 116:2; 1 John 5:14-15; Psalm 18:6; Galatians 6:9; Ephesians 1:3; Jeremiah 29:11; 2 Peter 3:8-9; Ephesians 3:20

Prayer of Praise: I thank you, Lord, that no matter what situation I'm in, I don't have to lose heart. I thank you that I can, will, and do believe that I will see your goodness in the land of the living. In fact, I am experiencing it today simply because I am breathing. I praise you that every moment I breathe I can experience you. I speak your goodness into existence in my life. And I will praise you until I feel that goodness in every part of my life. I thank you for giving me the courage, confidence, and endurance to wait on you. Thank you for strengthening my heart, in Jesus' name! Thank you, God! Thank you, God, for giving me yet another reason to praise! Amen.

Where have you lost heart and why?

_____

_____

_____

_____

_____

_____

_____

_____

_____

Write out Psalm 27:14.

_____

_____

_____

_____

Does having to wait evoke any negative emotions in you? If so, what are they? Share them with God.

_____

_____

_____

_____

_____

_____

_____

_____

_____

_____

_____

_____

God promised He'll strengthen you to endure and give you exceedingly abundantly above all that you could ask or think. Take the time to ask God to forgive you in any areas you lacked faith and trust His grace is sufficient for you.

Now, list some of the things you are expecting and hoping from God below.

_____

_____

_____

_____

_____

_____

_____

_____

_____

_____

_____

_____

_____

_____

_____

_____

_____

_____

_____

_____

I pray that you allow for Him to widen your perspective so that you'll receive the answered prayer, even if it doesn't look how you initially thought it would.

Day Sixteen
My Confidence Is in Him

For the Lord will be your confidence, and will keep your foot from being caught.

-Proverbs 3:26

What a blessing it is to be able to put our confidence and trust in God. What a blessing it is for God to let us know that He will be our confidence. When I saw this Scripture I was elated because it was an answer to a quick breath prayer I let out moments prior. I let God know that I wanted to have greater confidence in myself, and He reminded me that He is where my confidence should lie.

When God has trusted you with people's lives (whether you're a parent, teacher, leader, etc.), trusted you with the storms that you are walking through, or trusted you with the task of bringing others to Him (which we are all called to do) it can be a tad overwhelming, especially if you're attempting to do it all in your own strength.

All of us have been called to greater. All of us have been given gifts and are expected to fully utilize them. However, when you have had moments that feel like failure or have allowed people's opinions make you feel less than, it is hard to walk in confidence. When you have tried and tried to make certain things work, and they don't, it does something to your confidence. But at the end of the day, you don't have to rely on your own strength and abilities because while you have them both, God maximizes them to complete the task He has given to you.

God says He will be our confidence. That means we can rest on Him and His abilities with assurance. We know there is nothing too hard for God. He can do all things, and we can be strengthened to do all things through Him. So why do we doubt when God gives us a task?

Probably because we automatically take on His work when all we have to do is get in His word, listen to what He wants to share with us, and be obedient. We don't need to do any extras. All we need to do is what He said, and He'll handle the rest.

If He tells you to pray or encourage someone, you say what He says, and that's it. You don't babysit it. You don't try to make the word relevant for them. You don't do any of the work that God has planned to do. Be confident in His ability to be God and you allow yourself to be you.

We are working through God's power, we are working under His license, and He is willing to teach us all things and be the strength in every weak spot if we let Him!

We can praise God that we don't have to depend on ourselves or our abilities for everything we do. We can praise God that He has begun a good work in each and every one of us, and He will do what He set out to do.

It's not about what we can do. Praise Him for that. It's not about how perfect and special we are. Praise Him for that. It's not about how many times we've succeeded in the past, how many degrees we have, how many years we've been saved, or how many times we've missed the mark. Praise Him for that!

May our confidence be solely in our Creator. He is the only one who can speak a word, and it does not return void. Let us trust that every promise spoken over our lives and every gift imparted into our bodies **shall accomplish** what God pleases, and it shall prosper. We will prosper in all that we do. Even if it doesn't look like it, we know God can work all things out for the good. Can you be confident in that?

You don't have to worry about being confident in your abilities especially if God is calling you out of your comfort zone. The

Scripture says, ***Trust in the Lord with all your heart, and lean not on your own understanding*** (Proverbs 3:5). You can trust God! You can put your confidence in Him.

To God be the glory for the areas of your life that you do feel confident and walk with boldness in. And to God be the glory for those areas of your life that you feel weak and have to rest in His strength. Go in the confidence of the Lord today and praise Him for being all you need to accomplish every task set in front of you no matter how small or massive. It's all Him. Be confident in Him and praise Him because it's already done!

Scriptures: Proverbs 3:26; Jeremiah 32:27; Genesis 18:14; Philippians 4:13; John 14:26; Philippians 1:6; Isaiah 55:11; Romans 8:28; Proverbs 3:5

Prayer of Praise: God I thank you that I can allow my confidence to come strictly from you. I thank you that you are my confidence. It shows me another level of your love and grace that can't be explained or obtained by works. I thank you that when I fall short, I can be confident that you will pick up and accomplish the very task that you set out to fulfill. I thank you that I can do all things through you. I thank you that you can teach me everything I need to know to carry out the tasks that you have set before me today and the ones that will come tomorrow. I thank you that worry no longer has to be my best friend because I will now place my confidence and hope in you, the one true, consistent, stable, and living God that will keep my foot from getting caught. Thank you, God! Thank you, God, for giving me yet another reason to praise! In Jesus' name, amen.

What are three areas of your life you can work on trusting God a little more?

_____

_____

_____

_____

_____

_____

Don't know how to carry out the trusting part? That's normal. Ask God. He'll show you. You can either search how others did it in Scripture, pray for Him to lead you to people who have been where you are, or list a few ways you think you can attempt letting go today. Which will you do? Write them below as a reminder.

What Scriptures can help you gain confidence in God? Find a few and write them here. Take some time to meditate on them today.

_____

_____

_____

_____

_____

_____

_____

_____

_____

_____

_____

_____

Write a prayer asking God to help you increase your confidence in Him.

_____

_____

_____

_____

_____

_____

_____

_____

_____

_____

Make a list of a few ways you can begin the process of letting go and trusting God.

_____

_____

_____

_____

_____

_____

_____

_____

_____

_____

_____

_____

_____

_____

_____

_____

Day Seventeen
He Lifts Me From the Slimy Pit

"He also brought me up out of a horrible pit, Out of the miry clay, And set my feet upon a rock, And established my steps."

-Psalms 40:2

One of the worst feelings is being in a dark and low place. Sometimes we don't even realize we are there but when we do we begin to scramble to find a way out. We call out, we cry, we try our friends, or we try our favorite hang out spots as we search for a rope to grab so that we can pull ourselves out, but all of our devices seem to go unheard by God.

Then there are some of us that don't have the energy to fight, no energy to pray, praise, or read even a bit of Scripture. The little that comes up from the hidden places in our hearts have power, but we lack the faith at the time to activate them in our lives. I've been in both places before. And what the word says is true, it's horrible!

I've heard that the best thing you can do if you're ever caught in quicksand is to remain calm. I've also heard that when someone is struggling to stay afloat in water, it's not wise to assist them if their arms and legs are flailing as it puts both of you in danger. So here's what we need to do, rest.

Rest in the pit? Yes! God is there too. He can pull you out. But if you are struggling, swinging, or are even sitting still in defeat then you cannot see that He is standing with His arms open to carry you out. The praise part is that God can bring us out of the most horrible pit!

This Psalm was written by David. I mean, have you read his story? You have to. It will be an encouragement to you. God brought him out of a pit and set his feet on a rock. He was able to pull David out of every situation that he went through and not only help him get back on his feet, but He also spoke to him and gave him direction on how to move forward. What a blessing.

Whether you feel that you are in a pit, or God has delivered you from one, give Him praise simply because He can lift us out of every pit situation. Thank Him in advance for your deliverance and don't forget to thank Him for the last pit He pulled you out of. As God did with Joseph in Genesis, let Him use your pit situation to elevate you and put you in the position to save the lives of many others. Praise Him because He desires to see His children blessed with joy and peace. That goes for you too.

Scriptures: Psalm 40:2; Deuteronomy 31:6; Genesis 50:20

Prayer of Praise: God, I thank you for this pit situation. I thank you because I know you are producing something great from it and that it will help to save the lives of many. God, I thank you that although I've opened my eyes and found myself here that you are more than willing to pull me out, set my feet on solid ground, and establish my steps in you. I thank you that you have pulled me out of other pit situations whether I caused them from my disobedience or others caused them due to their hatred for the God that is on the inside of me. I thank you that you are with me at all times and if I stop wrestling, that I will find safety in your arms. Thank you, God! Thank you, God, for giving me yet another reason to praise! In Jesus' name, amen.

Pits, they do suck, and sometimes it feels too hard to come out of many of them. But there's hope. To begin your journey out of these pits, you have to choose whether or not you want to get out. It starts with your mindset.

Do you believe you have to be stuck there? _____

You don't!

Do you feel like there is no way out?_____

There is!

Identify your pit(s):

_____
_____
_____
_____
_____
_____
_____

What are three things you can do to begin climbing your way out mentally, physically, spiritually?

Example:
Mentally: Change my thought with the promise in Psalm 40:2.
Physically: Reach out to someone safe and share what I am feeling.
Spiritually: Pray specifically regarding this situation.

_____
_____
_____

Day Eighteen
His Grace Is All I Need

And He said to me, "My grace is sufficient for you, for My strength is made perfect in weakness." Therefore most gladly I will rather boast in my infirmities, that the power of Christ may rest upon me.

-2 Corinthians 12:9

We all have moments that we feel weak. All of us. There are moments that we don't want to do what God called us to because we believe we won't be good enough. We fear the failures of times past and even the failures that we have witnessed in other people's lives and avoid the tasks that God has placed on our hearts. Then there are those of us who have to deal with chronic health issues, or mental health issues, or any health issue. For every single thing you can think of, God's word remains true for you. His strength is made perfect in weakness.

I don't care where you feel you have a deficit. God is the answer. If He has called you to do something, He will provide you with every resource you need to carry it out. Every resource. Do you hear me? EVERY RESOURCE! Whether it is an external resource or the internal strength you need to believe in yourself and move forward, if God has called you to something, He will give you what you need to walk victoriously through it.

I am reminded of moments God called me to things greater than me. It seems to happen every day. One morning, in particular, stands out and was the inspiration for this devotion entry. I was preparing to start another semester of seminary. I had been away for a little while, so it was a big step getting back into the game. All of a sudden, I didn't feel good enough and briefly considered not going forward.

By this point, I had already obtained degrees, so I knew that it wasn't "the school" thing in general. My grades for previous semesters were all A's, but I was reminded of all of the well-versed Bible scholars, the difficulty of the curriculum, and having to make up for what I didn't know being new to Biblical studies unlike a majority of my cohort. I became overwhelmed with feeling weak, less than, and inferior.

Not even two hours later I got a text from a member of my church that included 2 Corinthians 12:9, a Scripture I meditated on a few days prior. God was reminding me that His grace extends to a multitude of needs and at that moment I needed to be reminded that in the place I felt weak (incapable, timid, lacking strength) that His grace was more than enough!

Surprisingly it gave me all I needed to remember that I was in His will, and I would be okay. I would be okay because everything isn't a cakewalk even if the degrees prior seemed to be easy as pie.

Honest moment: Sometimes it takes me a little more time to find peace with things.

I am reminded of the times I had to push and do what God had called me to do in sickness, whether physical, emotional, or spiritual, and how God came through in all His glory to accomplish the task that He set out for me. Remember, our confidence is in God, and He is able to do exceedingly abundantly above all that we could ever ask or think! We can have confidence that He will carry out every task and word spoken over and into our lives because that's what He promised. Your condition will not stunt what God wants to do in your life unless you let it!

So today I ask that instead of worrying if you can accomplish the task, that you praise God that His grace is all you need. It is indeed sufficient for you. He helped you do something new and difficult before and He can help you do it again. You just have to trust Him and praise Him all the way through.

Scriptures: 2 Corinthians 12:9; Ephesians 3:20; Philippians 1:6; Isaiah 55:11

Prayer of Praise: God, I thank you that all that I do really has nothing to do with me besides my obedience. I thank you that in areas I feel I fall short and where I actually fall short, that your grace is sufficient for me! Thank you for loving me so much that you provide everything I need to carry out the tasks you have set before me. God, I thank you for your grace! I thank you that it is a gift unto me. I thank you that my faith has made me whole in your grace! I thank you that it is all that I need! Thank you, God! Thank you, God, for giving me yet another reason to praise! In Jesus' name, amen.

In what areas are you feeling weak?

_____

_____

_____

_____

_____

_____

_____

Look at 2 Corinthians 12:9. What does it say?

God says my _____is_____
My_____is made_____in
_____.

What does this mean to you in relation to the weaknesses you listed above? Tell God about it:

_____

_____

_____

_____

_____

_____

_____

_____

_____

_____

_____

_____

_____

Even in weakness, you are strong! Say what?!
I know! God is just that good!

Day Nineteen
I Can Praise Him in Everything

In everything give thanks; for this is the will of God in Christ Jesus for you.

- 1 Thessalonians 5:18

Isn't it crazy to know we have to give thanks in everything we are going through? It may feel a little out of place in our lives at times, but we have to remember that praise is our weapon. It is one of those healthy distractions that puts us in communion with the Lord our Savior.

When we keep our mind stayed on God, we are promised peace. When we thank God for what He is doing in our lives and what He has done, we are lifting up the very One that created us and loves us.

We might not always like what we are going through, but we also know that God can and will work everything out for the good of those who love Him and are called according to His purpose. Seasons change, and as we learn in Ecclesiastes 3, there is a season for everything. Life and death, planting and plucking, killing and healing, breaking down and building up, weeping and laughing, mourning and dancing, throwing things out and gathering them, embracing and refraining, gaining and losing, keeping and throwing out, tearing and sewing, speaking and remaining quiet, loving and hate, times of war and times of peace.

There will always be seasons where we feel down, but this does not mean that God is any less good. Matter of fact, what makes Him great is that we can *still* praise in these down seasons. What makes Him greater is He has given us Scripture after Scripture teaching us how to remain encouraged in these seasons. He has given us example after example of other men and women in the Bible that went through the roughest pits and still survived. He has given us the ultimate example in the person of Jesus Christ.

I know that things don't always feel great, but praise should always be an option. In Psalm 34, David said, *I will bless the Lord at all times; His praise shall continually be in my mouth!*

At all times!

I don't believe this means you have to be up dancing, singing, and jumping around all the time, but I do believe that those moments where you just become aware of the goodness of God and think, "thank you" counts. I know that when you quickly say, "Thank you Jesus" or "I trust you Lord" He is pleased that you are thinking of Him in the midst of your troubles.

God is a very present help in the time of trouble, and one way of connecting with Him is through praise. So don't refrain from giving Him the glory He is due. Whether it is a loud shout, quiet whisper, tear-filled eyes, writing down what you are grateful for, or clapping your hands. Let your praise come out and gain the peace you deserve in the good and the bad.

Let everything that has breath praise the Lord!

Scriptures: 1 Thessalonians 5:18; Isaiah 26:3; Romans 8:28; Ecclesiastes 3:1-8; Psalm 34:1; Psalm 46:1; Psalm 150:6

Prayer of Praise: Although it is hard at times I thank you that I can praise you at all times and that you will be near me, receive me, and that I will feel your peace. I thank you that my praise is innate to me and can connect me with you in marvelous ways. Today I thank you in all that I am going through knowing that you will work all things out for the good of those who love you and are called according to your purpose! I thank you for what you have done in my life. I thank you for what you are doing now, and I thank you for all that you will do in my tomorrow! Thank you, God! Thank you, God, for giving me yet another reason to praise! In Jesus' name, amen.

Read Philippians 4:8.

List all of the praiseworthy things in your life:

_____

_____

_____

_____

_____

_____

_____

_____

_____

_____

_____

_____

_____

_____

_____

_____

_____

_____

_____

_____

_____

Praise God for them throughout today and at the end of the day, I want you to reflect and see if your peace was steadier than on a day that you were not focused on praise.

Day Twenty
The Rain Has Purpose

Sing to the Lord with thanksgiving; Sing praises on the harp to our God, Who covers the heavens with clouds, who prepares rain for the earth, who makes grass to grow on the mountains.

- Psalm 147:7-8

We have to be mindful of our thoughts throughout the day. In the moments that we are alone, and it's quiet, it's imperative that we continue to think positively. Many people avoid silence because of the thoughts and emotions that arise during that time. You start to think about the things you lack, the things that have hurt you, and the mistakes you have made. But, keeping our eyes stayed on Jesus by singing songs of thanksgiving are what will help us move quickly past those moments and allow for God to lead us through our day filled with joy.

When I read this Scripture, it was at a point where I needed God to *reign* and *rain* in my life. I wanted Him to have complete and total control, and I also desired for Him to release His blessings. So in this particular Scripture, the words *rain* and *grow* stuck out to me. However, my previous actions made me feel unworthy of the positive rain. I started looking at the storms I was facing as punishment.

God reminded me that I was being showered with His love in a myriad of ways. This included discipline. The Scripture says He chastens those He loves. Not to demean but to help us grow. While God loves us dearly, there are consequences we face due to our poor decisions or indecisions. I thought of what I was facing because of poor choices and realized this was indeed a sort of blessed rain. In spite of me and my low moments, He was continuously pouring out His grace, mercy, and other spiritual blessings that kept me during that time. Blessings and grace I didn't believe I deserved, but He supplied freely.

Whenever it rains the water saturates the land making it ready for increase. After the rain the air smells different, the flowers are set to bloom, and dry lands in need are filled with moisture to provide life for the humans and animals that inhabit it. Whatever God allows to rain on us, we can trust that it will make us grow in some way.

God will use all things for the good if you love Him and are called according to His purpose. So even if it's a storm or the consequences that come with that storm that are raining on you right now, you have to praise God!

God can stop anything He wants to stop so if He is allowing the good and the bad to happen in your life we have to remember that it's just like fertilizer prepping the seed on the inside of us for growth. You might not see the results right away but know that God is working. And when He gets to work it's always amazing. What He creates is good. Every good and perfect gift comes from God, even the stuff that appears to come from a jumbled mess!

Allow the rain in your life, both the lovely and unpleasant to fall where it may, praise Him in the storm, and understand that your anointing is increasing as you do. It's the anointing that destroys the yokes of bondage. Let the rain come and make you and everyone around you better.

Scriptures: Psalm 147:7-8; Hebrews 12:6; Proverbs 3:12; Romans 8:28; James 1:17; Isaiah 10:27

Prayer of Praise: God I thank you for the rain in my life. Sometimes I don't like being drenched. It's uncomfortable and cold, but I thank you for being warmth in the midst. God, I also thank you for the pleasant rain. I know that you can build and grow in both, and I look forward to what it is you are cultivating in my life that I may reach out and touch the lives of others by sharing your goodness. Thank you for the rain! Thank you for keeping me in the rain! Thank you, God! Thank you, God, for giving me yet another reason to praise! In Jesus' name, amen.

Where has God reigned or rained in your life and you saw the increase that came from it?

_____

_____

_____

_____

_____

_____

If He did it before, He will do it again.

Can't find an example? Ask God to reveal it and as soon as He does, write it down.

Can you trust God in your rainy season(s)?

_____

_____

_____

What are some praiseworthy things that can come from this rainy season? Call them out right now:

_____

_____

_____

_____

_____

_____

_____

_____

_____

_____

Day Twenty-One
Laughter Is a Blessing

A merry heart does good, like medicine, but a broken spirit dries the bones.

-Proverbs 17:22

A cheerful heart is good medicine, but a broken spirit saps a person's strength.

-Proverbs 17:22 NLT

Have you ever experienced a hearty laugh? Like the kind that leads to tears, a pain in your side, and maybe even the inability to breathe? Think about how you feel after those moments. Praiseworthy don't you think? There's a freedom in it, there's a release, there's relief! It causes one to forget about all of the things that could have been burdening them that day.

I love to laugh! I'm the kind of person who will bust up laughing at some of the things that happen in the Bible (these people were crazy), or laugh at songs that are meant to be serious, or just have a personal thought and fall out laughing. I often apologize when this happens but I shouldn't. Why? Because a merry heart does good like medicine and to keep it real, I'm in need of medicine often.

I've watched people in hospital beds get tickled by a joke and for that moment, although they are begging for you not to make them laugh, they get to escape from a place of their natural disposition and go somewhere healthy and safe. Moments of laughter are definitely reasons to praise!

But what about those times where you are in a pit and can't seem to find anything funny? What about those moments where laughter is desired but can't be obtained? Praise Him for it anyways! Praise God for the laughter and good times that have made your heart merry in the past. Or if you have never experienced this rush of excitement, praise Him for how you can experience it in your now and your future.

The Bible says that we can speak those things that aren't as if they already are. Speak laughter, good conversation, and funny moments into your life. Praise God and don't be surprised if this burst of laughter overtakes you even if no jokes have been told. God wants to see you cheerful and merry because the alternative is dried up bones. He's about life, and dry bones are not abundant living!

So today, praise your way into a cheerful heart. Praise your way into laughter. Reach out to someone who always makes you laugh (that's a goal of mine to do at least weekly), watch a comedy, or just get out and be silly. It will take you a long way. It will ease hurt, and it will give you a safe escape into another realm of God's love.

Laugh your way through today!

Scriptures: Proverbs 17:22; Romans 4:17; John 10:10; Nehemiah 8:10

Prayer of Praise: Lord, I thank you for laughter! I thank you for the funny moments, the cheerful moments, and those moments I am only able to laugh at in retrospect. God, I thank you that you have created a healthy way for us to deal with things in life. I thank you that I can find happiness in you and that you are okay with laughter. Today I will laugh my way through every situation, I will praise my way into laughter, and I will experience your joy, which just so happens to be my strength! I declare that there will be no dry bones in me on today! Even if I don't feel like it, Lord, cause me to laugh today. I love you and thank you in advance! Thank you, God! Thank you, God, for giving me yet another reason to praise! In Jesus' name, amen.

How does laughter make you feel?

_____

_____

_____

List three ways you can get a surefire laugh today, even if you have to do it alone.

_____

_____

_____

_____

_____

_____

_____

_____

Anything else?

_____

_____

_____

_____

_____

_____

_____

_____

_____

_____

_____

Day Twenty-Two
I Can Do Anything Through Him

I can do all things through Christ who strengthens me.
- Philippians 4:13

It's very easy to be discouraged when things get rough. When we come up against a problem or task that feels like it's entirely too much to handle alone or even as a family or team, we can praise God because He promises us that we can do all things through Him.

Do you trust God? Do you have confidence that if He brought you to something that He will provide you with all the tools necessary to complete the task? Even if that tool is patience, remaining quiet instead of running your mouth, or stepping out on faith, can you trust God for perfect provision?

God is willing to be the main driving force in your life if you let Him. If you can trust that He will strengthen you to complete the task set before you, you will see your life overflow with an abundance of Him!

Scripture tells us that God is in control, and there is nothing too hard for Him (Jeremiah 33:27). Do you trust that? Doesn't it make something in your spirit jump to know that the Creator of the universe and your soul, who nothing is too hard for, will give you the strength to face every situation happening in your life? Doesn't it please you to know that you are victorious in Him no matter what it looks like?

So today I encourage you to praise God because His strength is given to you in all situations! Knowing that, I beseech you, *you like that word huh?* I highly encourage you to go ye therefore and do what God has called you to do on this day, at this moment.

Remember there is nothing too hard for you to do through Him. He will give you the strength to face all that you go through. He will even give you strength to deal with the consequences of your disobedience. He is just good like that. When He's ready to move forward with you, He does just that.

He is ready to do something new in you! You just have to build up the confidence in Him to take the next step forward. Can you go to the next level in your faith and believe and trust God even in this? Trust Him. He can do exceedingly above all that you could ever ask of Him or think.

It's important that you remember to lean on His promise when things seem too huge or far too hard. God is more than willing to provide you with a way of escape to handle all situations, but you have to turn to Him to get it. One of these ways is through faith in His word. Read that thang! Another is through praise. Send up your words of gratitude as often as you can and watch Him take over and show out!

Knowing you are strengthened in God to complete every task set before you is *definitely* a reason to praise!

Scriptures: Philippians 4:13; Jeremiah 33:27; Matthew 28:19; Isaiah 43:19; Ephesians 3:20; 1 Corinthians 10:13; Romans 8:37

Prayer of Praise: God I thank you that through you I can do all things. When a problem that appears to be bigger than I am arises, I will surrender it to you knowing that there is nothing too hard for you. I will stop stressing over things that you have already promised to handle. I will walk with a victorious disposition because I am more than a conqueror! God today show me every way of escape, so I can bear everything I will deal with today.

Thank you in advance for handling every situation! Thank you for doing something new in me! Thank you for giving me the strength I need to walk forward in my calling today, even if it's simply smiling at a stranger. I love you God, and I thank you! Thank you, God! Thank you, God, for giving me yet another reason to praise! In Jesus' name, amen.

If we are real, I think we can all admit to having spoken the words, "I can't." It could have been, I can't gather the confidence to try that new thing, I can't be used for such a great task, I can't get that job, I can't get out of bed today, I can't deal with that person or issue, I can't afford it financially, I can't afford it time wise, or simply, I just can't.

Well, I want you to list your *"I can't"* thoughts for this day. Get them out of you!

_____

_____

_____

_____

_____

_____

_____

Now take one (or more) that are the heaviest on you and use Philippians 4:13 to:
1) Speak life
2) Encourage yourself
3) Immobilize the devil (he has to subject himself to the word of God)

I can _____ because Christ gives me the strength to do it!

I can _____ because Christ gives me the strength to do it!

It might seem crazy, but such a simple phrase can do some heavy work in your life. Don't forget to use it!

Day Twenty-Three
His Word is His Word

Your word is a lamp to my feet and a light to my path.

-Psalm 119:105

The word of God is one of the greatest reasons to praise we've been given. Have you ever heard or read a Scripture that spoke to your life in such a way that it completely changed you? Have you ever sat in a church and heard the preacher teach from a text, and have you looking around like, "How'd they know that?"

God's word is alive, and it is active in our lives. Do you hear me? It is living, and it's powerful! Someone may think, how can the Bible be living?

This God-inspired text has been given to us to teach us, correct us, and train us so that we are equipped for all that God has called us to. In this word, we learn about His truths, His love, His grace, His desire to prosper us and not harm us, His desire to be in true and real relationship with us, and His desire to come back for those who love Him that we may spend eternity with Him.

In this word we see situations from thousands of years ago speak to what we are dealing with today. In the Scriptures He so graciously left us, we are inspired in several different ways with the same text. Take Psalm 119:105 for example. At one point in my life, I lacked direction. Although I was already done with college and in graduate school, I didn't know what God was calling me to do. I knew what I was good at doing, but that wasn't fulfilling. I knew what I loved but that, well that didn't promise to pay the bills (which I've learned doesn't matter). I needed God to show me what He needed from me. I needed God to show me what He purposed me to do. So as I sat in the word of God He began to illuminate my path. He began to show me my gifts and talents and made me recognize real life examples in my daily interactions with people. He lit the path so I could find Him and then find out who I was in Him.

Then I had moments where this Scripture spoke to me differently. I've had many dark, dark...*dark* moments in my life. The word was the only thing that got me through. Even when I couldn't open my Bible, I had people speak the Scriptures into my spirit. Those words illuminated the path towards His light and led me back to Him and back on track.

This one Scripture, at two different times in my life, spoke to me differently. It inspired me in the way it needed to while staying within the proper context. God's word is living because God is about life. He knows that a dead text can't transcend generations as it has. Allow the word to flow through your life and touch your current situation.

Praise God that He has given us a way to understand Him and ourselves through Him. Praise Him that we don't have to walk blindly but that His word can lead and guide us in everything that we do!

Scriptures: Psalm 119:105; Hebrews 4:12; 2 Timothy 3:16-17

Prayer of Praise: Thank you for the word of God. Thank you for leaving us instructions meant to teach, inspire, correct, and prepare us. Thank you that everything I could ever go through is covered in the text. I thank you that your word is alive and a powerful force in my life. I pray that I will use it to battle every situation I face in my life. I pray that I will use it to learn more about your love so that I can love you, myself, and others properly. Thank you for giving us the hope we need in Jesus and that we can learn all about it in this word. May it continue to be a lamp unto my feet and a light to my path. Thank you, God! Thank you, God, for giving me yet another reason to praise! In Jesus' name amen.

Recall can be good for the soul's journey. How has the word been a lamp to your feet?

_____

_____

_____

_____

_____

_____

_____

_____

What are you looking for in the word now?

_____

_____

_____

_____

_____

_____

_____

How will you get that today?

_____

_____

_____

_____

_____

_____

_____

_____

JOURNAL

Day Twenty-Four
My Thoughts Can Change My Life

Guard your heart above all else, for it determines the course of your life.

-Proverbs 4:23 NLT

I have to take a minute and praise God for clear instructions! I have to praise Him for teaching me that if we can get our minds to focus on Him and the good things, we can change the entire course of our lives.

In the Scripture, it says to guard your heart above all else! This needs to be a top priority, and it's obvious as to why. Think about when you get angry or get your feelings hurt, or you fear that the worst will happen and how that causes you to act and treat others. It's not usually positive.

Someone may be wondering why in the world I would translate the word heart to thoughts. Well in this context we can look at the word heart to mean, someone's inner self, their inclination, disposition, determination, courage, will, intention, attention, consideration, their place of reason.[1] Just about everything we do starts in the heart.

God is asking us to protect everything about us! If we know that something doesn't line up with the will of God for our lives, we need to run! Resist so that the devil will flee and doesn't have an opportunity to get us to change the course of our lives for the worse.

A reason to praise is that you can change your thinking, what you choose to be intent on, what you choose to consider, what you're inclined to focus on. In doing so you can change the course of your day, week, month, year, and life. You can change the course of your emotions causing for more stability in spite of what you may be feeling.

If you don't know what to think, or perhaps you find yourself wanting to dwell on the very things causing you to go in a negative direction, you can praise God that He gave you directions on what to think about that can be found in Philippians 4:8.

The word of God also teaches us how to use those thoughts to destroy the negative ones. In 2 Corinthians 10:5, in the New Living Translation, it says, *We destroy every proud obstacle that keeps people from knowing God. We capture their rebellious thoughts and teach them to obey Christ.*

Every thought leading you away from Christ should be captured and replaced with Scripture. When you are feeling a way that you know isn't right, find Scripture that encourages you and replace it with that. Praise God for His truth that brings light and life and takes the place of the lies that are causing darkness and death in your life. Praise God for the freedom that can be found by guarding our hearts.

Scriptures: Proverbs 4:23 NLT; James 4:7; Philippians 4:8; 2 Corinthians 10:5

Prayer of Praise: God, I thank you for the word that convicts my flesh and helps me stay in line with your will. I thank you for the word that's readily available to help us not only fight our battles but helps us change the entire course of our lives. Today, I pray for your help to be diligent in replacing any negative thoughts with the truth of your word! I thank you for giving me such a powerful tool to protect and guard my heart so the course of my life reflects your love, mercy, and grace. Thank you, God! Thank you, God, for giving me yet another reason to praise! In Jesus' name amen.

What are some areas of your heart you need to guard today and why?

_____

_____

_____

_____

_____

_____

When we point these things out, they tend to magnify for us. Not because they are any worse, but because we've just put our attention on them. So, be prepared by answering the following questions.

Who are some people you can contact if you need support?

_____

_____

_____

_____

Read 2 Corinthians 10:5 again.

What are some Scriptures you can use if your heart begins to feel threatened?

_____

_____

_____

_____

_____

_____

_____

What/who should you avoid?

_____

_____

_____

_____

_____

_____

_____

_____

_____

_____

Anything else?

_____

_____

_____

_____

_____

_____

_____

_____

_____

_____

Stay ready, and don't forget to use 2 Corinthians 10:5.

Day Twenty-Five
He Knows What I Need

That is why I tell you not to worry about everyday life—whether you have enough food and drink, or enough clothes to wear. Isn't life more than food, and your body more than clothing? Look at the birds. They don't plant or harvest or store food in barns, for your heavenly Father feeds them. And aren't you far more valuable to him than they are? Can all your worries add a single moment to your life?

-Matthew 6:25-27 NLT

Today's devotion is very similar to day five, but sometimes we need the extra encouragement!

In this passage, I see God telling us that we don't have to worry about one solitary thing in our lives. God cares about us, and He desires to meet our needs.

Verse 25 tells us do not worry about everyday life. That's everything that makes up every facet of our life. From the way that we move, breathe, and have our being, to the things we need to survive, to the emotional and physical needs that present themselves daily.

God knows when you're hungry, when your bank account is low, when there's no gas in your car, or when you don't feel like you have enough fuel to get through the day. He knows when you need peace or to reclaim your joy. He knows when you need an embrace from a safe person, He knows when you need a rhema, or on time spoken word, which could likely save your life. He knows!

His understanding of you and every other creation is infinite. He gets it even when we don't. And He is more than willing to provide and meet all of our needs according to His riches in glory. He's got all we need and will provide all we need.

I've seen God handle all these things I listed and more in my life, in His own way.

God moves on our behalf in ways that we will know it's Him, and in ways we will feel His love radiate even if He's using a third party. God is the ultimate provider in every realm of our life: spiritually, emotionally, mentally, physically, financially, relationally—EVERY realm. So make your requests known to Him and let His peace rest over you so that you can maintain until you see the physical or spiritual manifestation of what you are asking for. Praise God because He knows your need, and praise God because He desires to meet those needs.

Let's take it a step further, praise Him because He actually *can* meet all those needs!

Scriptures: Matthew 6:25-34, Acts 17:28; Psalm 147:5; Philippians 4:19; Philippians 4:6-7

Prayer of Praise: God, I thank you for knowing every intimate detail of my life including my needs that don't matter to others but matter to me. I thank you for providing every need even if it's not in the way I expected. Today I will praise you for what I have, keeping my eyes on those praiseworthy things so that I can see you as the great God that you are instead of looking at my situation as if it's bigger than you. God, right now I make my requests known to you. I'm informing you of what I am in need of, and I am even open to you letting me know the difference between a need and want. I thank you for your love and for your desire to see me taken care of.

Today, I will not worry. I will praise! I will not wonder if things will get taken care of because I believe they already are. Thank you, God! Thank you, God, for giving me yet another reason to praise! In Jesus' name amen.

Ask yourself, are you valuable to God? Write your answer here.

_____

_____

If God takes care of the birds and flowers, then He will take care of you! Trust this promise.

List areas you feel you are lacking and are causing you to worry.

_____

_____

_____

_____

_____

_____

As you list your needs pray and believe that He will see about them and that you can trust as you wait.

If you want, you can write your prayer out here and then say it aloud. When you are finished, read your prayer of praise from today's devotion once again.

_____

_____

_____

_____

_____

_____

_____

_____

Day Twenty-Six
The Word Doesn't Change

The grass withers, the flower fades, But the word of our God stands forever.

-Isaiah 40:8

Praise God because the same word that led you to deliverance and positive change before remains the same. It can and will lead you back to a road of deliverance and positive change today.

Have you ever jumped over a hurdle, gotten over something, came through the fire, been delivered from something, someone, or someplace? Isn't it a magnificent feat? It feels so good to be on the other side of the problem and look back and start to gain some insight on why you were going through what you were going through. You praise God for the victory, and you keep it pushing.

One afternoon I had an experience where the very thing I thought I moved past was brought back to my attention in a way that let me know there was still more to be worked out. That day I experienced three different triggers that took me back to a place of anger, hurt, and even feelings of hate. These negative emotions attempted to fill my heart and pour out. So I cried out to God asking for His help. And when I say cry, I mean ugly cry.

Even in my hurt, even through my tears, there were a few things I was very aware of at the time. I knew for a fact that God had very well delivered me from this situation. I was no longer in it. I was no longer bound by it. This was just a moment that I could simply cast my cares over to Him or choose to dwell and drown in them. I had the choice! Unfortunately, it took me a couple of days to decide to cast my cares and move on.

I knew for a fact that I had moved forward in a level of healing, but obviously, there was something more. There was a gap that I missed, and God knew that this was the perfect time to look back and strengthen the areas that the enemy would still attempt to get through. I praised God because as I cried out to Him, He reminded me of every reason I had to praise. He brought to my remembrance every Scripture He used to pull me out and begin the healing process the first time and even showed me where those words were manifested in my life. I had to praise Him because His word endures forever and that same word that pulled me out times prior would pull me out now.

I was reminded to stay steadfast in the word, to seek peace and pursue it, and to resist the devil so he would flee. Sometimes it takes a little more than changing your thoughts once to save your peace of mind. I had to *keep* applying the word that worked for me yesterday and many times before. I had to capture those thoughts and bring them into the obedience of Christ *repeatedly*! This took work. I had to repeat this task throughout the day until I was able to believe it and apply it by moving on with my day instead of dwelling on the hurt.

So, whether the negative thing comes back up in your life or a new trial or storm slaps you in your throat and blindsides you, we can praise God that the word remains the same. It can still guide you and lead you into His perfect will. It can still prove to you that you can be healed. It can still give guidance on how to guard your heart and change your thoughts. It can still teach you about God's grace that is available to you in spite of the situation you find yourself in. It can still teach you that His love endures through anything that may happen, and nothing can separate you from it.

The same promise of peace still applies. The same promise of joy still applies. The same promise of strength and endurance still applies. The same promise of salvation still applies. The word is everlasting and endures forever. I don't care if your situation has changed. I don't care if your feelings have changed. I don't care if the enemy got in and has you feeling every way but godly. You have to praise God that His word is unchanging.

The same word that led you to deliverance in God before is the same word that can do that today. Nothing has changed except the way that you're responding. Praise God now and watch your life improve.

Scriptures: Isaiah 40:8; 1 Peter 5:7; 1 Peter 1:24-25; 1 Corinthians 15:58; Psalm 34:14; James 4:7

Prayer of Praise: Lord, I thank you that your word endures forever. I thank you that it is alive and powerful in my life and that it can be used for any and every situation I may face. I thank you that even when it feels like the word is no longer working in my life that you will guide me back to the very place that encouraged me before and prove to me, and my enemies, that it still works and will always work. I pray that I can apply your word in spite of how I feel because I believe in my heart and know without a doubt that it will work to empower me, teach me, and guide me in all your ways! I love you, and I thank you, God! Thank you, God, for giving me yet another reason to praise! In Jesus' name, amen.

What came up for you while reading this devotion? That's what you're going to focus on today. Write it out:

_____

_____

_____

_____

_____

_____

_____

_____

What Scriptures do you already know that can help you get through this rough moment? Write them here:

_____

_____

_____

_____

_____

_____

_____

_____

Meditate on these Scriptures and allow them to lead you to new places in the word.

Use them today.

You are an overcomer, and because you have access to God and His word, the victory is no doubt yours.

Have a great day! Praise Him!

Day Twenty-Seven
He Can Quench My Thirst

But whoever drinks of the water that I shall give him will never thirst. But the water that I shall give him will become in him a fountain of water springing up into everlasting life.

- John 4:14

We all have experienced a longing for something. More than likely it's a type of love, security, and freedom that we are looking for. We search everywhere to quench this thirsting of our souls, but the problem is that often, we are only meeting the needs of our flesh.

According to this Scripture, we can conclude that this love, this security, this hope, this freedom, this life-giving high that we are seeking can only come from Christ. This is the reason that we should praise. Many of us have been searching for years and years to find what will fill the voids in our lives and here the word of God tells us exactly where this need can be met. At His well! If we drink from Him, we will never thirst again.

Now some of you may think what I have thought plenty of times, "If the word says that we will never thirst again, why am I so thirsty now?" Jesus has made Himself available to us. However, we must choose to drink from Him daily. We must choose to be consistent in coming to His well because the enemy is going to consistently provide us with many poisonous alternatives. He is going to be consistent in providing us with ways of the world to distract us from drinking from the only well of lasting satisfaction. So as temptations arise, we can praise God that we don't need to fall into the enemy's traps because Jesus has already given us our fill.

Anytime you are feeling thirsty or have found yourself removed you can go back to Him. Just as you would go back to get another high, or call the person on the phone that you miss dearly, or back to a casino to feel the rush, you can go back to our Heavenly Father to get all that you need in one safe and secure spot.

Invest in your relationship with God today to get what you need and to give Him what is necessary. We were created to be in relationship with God. He can't pour if we don't open up to Him to drink. Therefore, we must be open to receive and to reciprocate.

God loves you and is willing to satisfy you at all times. The love is unconditional and without fault. He loves you even when you miss His call. He understands every bit of you without you having to say a word. His love is unfailing and again unconditional. He chooses to love every intricate part of you. He can and will deal with you on your worst days and is still there at your best. He has your best interests at heart and totally believes in you even when you doubt Him. He knows your weaknesses and still lets you rest in Him. He gives you confidence in His strength, which makes you stronger because you are connected to Him. He is perfect, so great, so mighty, that even the winds and sea obey His command. God is the lover of your soul and can be all you need to satisfy the yearning you have to be loved, feel loved, and receive love.

So praise Him for being willing to quench the thirsting of your soul and then trust Him with the part of you that is parched and seeking respite in the very things that pull you away from Him. Let Him be your everything.

Scriptures: John 4:14; Romans 8: 31-39; Psalm 147:5; 2 Corinthians 12:9-11; Matthew 8:27

Prayer of Praise: God, I thank you for showing me the desires of my heart all lead back to you. I thank you for every blessing in my life, but I am most grateful for the spiritual blessings of your grace and love. I thank you that you are willing to quench the thirsting of my soul. I repent for trying everything and anything to fix this issue of drought from within, and I pray that you will teach me how to drink from your well and your well alone. I thank you for loving all of me at all times. I thank you that I can come to you in my truth and that you are still willing to empty me of every bad thing and fill me with you. I thank you for this process even if it hurts, even if the withdrawals are uncomfortable, even if I want to give up and go back. I thank you that you are my strength when I am weak. I love you, and I thank you, God! Thank you, God, for giving me yet another reason to praise! In Jesus' name, amen.

We are all thirsting for something, and that's fine as long as we're drinking from the right well. Don't allow your blessings to become your god or your drink. We don't want you contaminated. Today I want you to list the areas in your life you are feeling thirsty and in need of a drink from Jesus' well.

_____

_____

_____

_____

_____

_____

_____

_____

Now write out how you can drink from God first so you won't consume poison in search of fulfillment that can only come from God.

_____

_____

_____

_____

_____

_____

_____

_____

_____

_____

_____

If you're not sure, don't give up. Pray and ask God for your help in filling this section out.

Day Twenty-Eight
He's There to Help & Lift Me

The Lord helps the fallen and lifts those bent beneath their loads.

-Psalm 145:14 NLT

Here's a portion of a journal entry where this Scripture became relevant in my life. I hope in sharing you will see another reason we have to praise.

"I've fallen back into a pit of despair. I picked up all the hurt and held it instead of casting it over to God. So it got heavier with each thought. And then the tears came. We know what happens when things get wet. They get heavier. So I was bent over by what I picked up. All I could think was my joy and peace was activated not even four days ago...Get back there; you know how. It's in the word. But the smokescreens seemed real. They seemed bigger than me and my will to get past them. I had to remind myself that the same word that delivered me last time will do it again. I just have to be diligent and put action behind what I believe. I want to be free to walk in my peace and freedom again."

It took me two weeks to hike to the top of that mountain of peace. It took me two weeks to get all my negative thoughts in alignment with God so that I wasn't fighting for my peace in that area. It felt great. It felt amazing actually! And then in one moment and a barrage of negative thoughts later, I found myself right back in the pit. Two weeks to hike to the top of the mountain and only two days to slide back down and feel stuck.

We can't be discouraged by the events that cause us to fall back into the pits we just made our way out of. Whatever that pit is, mental, emotional, physical, or spiritual we can definitely get back out.

If you've looked up and realize you have fallen back into depression or anxiety, back into the relationship God wants you out of, back into the addiction, back into that negative space, remember, **the Lord helps the fallen and lifts those bent beneath their loads.**

Take it as an opportunity to praise God for showing you that you even fell. Some people are so consumed in what they are in they miss the memo that they are in unsafe territory. So thank God for the revelation.

Take this as an opportunity to learn something new about yourself, about God, and about your strength in Him. There are always learning opportunities in all that we do. God can use everything for the good. You know this.

Take this moment as an opportunity to recognize the same word God gave you, the same weapons, and spiritual tactics that lifted you out the last time can lift you out this time. Not only can you come out but you now have the potential to do it in record time. You already know what to do! And although getting out may feel harder since going back you know the tools in your belt work. Trust them and use them.

Use this as an opportunity to praise God for the wisdom acquired to learn, recognize, and apply these Scriptures. You're still more than a conqueror. Still called according to His purpose. Still made strong in your weakness. Still created and called for a time such as this. The Lord desires to help you and even lift you if you let Him. Will you let Him today?

Go back to the basics of what you know in Him. Let Him lead you back to safe and solid ground. Praise Him in advance, all throughout the journey, and when you get back to the top of that mountain.

Scriptures: Psalm 145:14; Romans 8:37, 8:28; 2 Corinthians 12:9-11; Esther 4:14

Prayer of Praise: God, thank you for your faithfulness. I thank you that no matter what pit I find myself in that you are more than willing and more than capable to help me out and lift me up. Sometimes life circumstances overwhelm me, especially if I have not cast my cares on you. Well, today I thank you for still being the safe space I can lean on to lift me up, straighten me out, and take every burden I give to you! Thank you for the opportunity to realize where I was, thank you for teaching me something new, thank you for the unchanging word that you left just for me, and thank you for your wisdom given to me to get out of this pit. Thank you, God! Thank you, God, for giving me yet another reason to praise! In Jesus' name, amen.

What did this devotion and Scripture awaken in you? Share it with God:

_____

_____

_____

_____

_____

_____

_____

_____

_____

In today's devotion, I wrote, _"Take it as an opportunity to recognize the same word God gave you, the same weapons, and spiritual tactics that got you out the last time can get you out this time."_

What tools are already in your tool box? List them now and use them today.

_____

_____

_____

_____

_____

_____

_____

_____

_____

_____

_____

_____

_____

Day Twenty-Nine
It Will Be Better

'The glory of this latter temple shall be greater than the former,' says the Lord of hosts. 'And in this place I will give peace,' says the Lord of hosts.

-Haggai 2:9

Today, I'm writing to the person that fears that it might be time to transition. Although it might feel scary, difficult, and overwhelming, I encourage you to praise God that He has better for you even if you have to walk away from something familiar to get it.

It's not always about the people, places, or things being no good for you or so horrible that you must leave and move forward. Sometimes your transition to something new is simply because it's time. Time to move forward to get your blessings in a new way. These blessings include peace. If you lack peace, God will give you a place where it is waiting for you, but you have to be willing to move to get it. Whether it's you having a better thought life or having to literally move locations to receive the peace of the Lord, you've got to be willing to move.

I know, even the thought of loss can be overwhelming, but remember anything that you lose you can guarantee God will replace. It might not look shinier, but it will be exactly what you need. You might miss what you are leaving behind, but you can still love what you're leaving while moving on.

I loved my first car. If I could have kept it and upgraded, I would have, but I had to walk away from it to get important needs met; like being able to count on it starting without having to slam the trunk first. There were obviously some things the car could no longer do for me that needed to be done. Even still, it was hard to walk away. It was hard to clean it out and leave it at the car dealership knowing someone else would quite possibly grab all the benefits I once had. Even though I was driving off the lot with something new, my emotional attachment made it difficult for me.

I've had two cars since then and I still think about my first car. I also know that I don't need to go back to it, and at this point, I don't want to. The nostalgia is enough. While a car might not be that important to many people, it's a simple example of how there are times we have to move forward and be willing to lose a little to gain much more. I gained new standard options and a car that was going to get me through the rest of my college years and the commute involved. I got what I needed in that season to complete the task at hand.

So when we have to walk away from relationships, jobs, churches, social clubs, or even cars, whether they were toxic or not, we can praise God knowing He is going to take us somewhere that will be better for us in that season. It will be a place where all your needs are met and most importantly a place that He will give you peace.

Praise God that He is always willing to lead us to a place where our true needs and desires can be met for that moment, for that season. So go without fear because greater is necessary and that is what God will provide in your willing obedience. May your latter be greater than your former!

Scriptures: Haggai 2:9; Philippians 4:19

Prayer of Praise: Even if it hurts, God I want to thank you for thinking so much of me that you would take me from where I am and place me where I need to be to get every need in my life met.

I thank you that you will emotionally, spiritually, and physically prepare me for every place you are taking me if I allow for it. I pray for the peace to go without a fight and that I see you working all through the transition. I thank you for all of the transitions you have already brought me through and I praise you for taking care of me in those things because they lead me to know and believe that you will continue to do the same thing for me in this. Thank you for preparing a place and thank you for peace. Thank you, God! Thank you, God, for giving me yet another reason to praise! In Jesus' name, amen.

That thing that came to mind as you read today's devotion, yeah... that. It just might be an area God is trying to speak to you about. Does it mean that you're going to have to walk away from it? No, not necessarily but it's worth taking it to God in prayer.

I pray the wall that might have come up as you read the last few sentences will slide back down. I know the wall well. It's something we slide up to protect ourselves but many times it hinders us from receiving God's truth.

So when you're ready, write down what came up in your spirit. How do you feel about it? Is it an emotional or thought based transition? Or is it something you have to do physically? Write about it:

_____

_____

_____

_____

_____

_____

_____

List the pros and cons regarding it and the pros and cons related to staying with it or leaving it.

_____

_____

_____

_____

_____

_____

_____

Don't forget to take Scripture into account. Which ones are coming up in your spirit right now?

_____

_____

_____

_____

_____

_____

_____

_____

_____

_____

_____

_____

_____

Praise God for your better, whether your "it" will change altogether or be restored.

Trust God and praise Him!

Day Thirty
He's With Me Wherever I Go

Have I not commanded you? Be strong and of good courage; do not be afraid, nor be dismayed, for the LORD your God is with you wherever you go.

-Joshua 1:9

Many times God will call us to things that are bigger than us, way out of our comfort zone, or to do things that make our flesh cry out even though it would do wonders for our spiritual self. In these moments, it can be hard to praise God. Why? Because your flesh might be warring with your spirit telling it, "No, I don't want to go!" While your spirit is saying, "But this is the order from the Lord, we have to."

I've been there far too many times to count, and I don't always do well with the initial word to go forward if it means leaving what is familiar. I've been known to break down in tears, close my Bible, or shut down so that I don't hear, or flat out say, "No."

I don't write that so you feel that it's perfectly fine to do that because it's not. Where's the faith in that? Where is the confidence in the Lord who only has plans to give us a future and a hope? I shared my truth to say that we are human with human emotions and behaviors. The anxiety of moving forward happens, but God still loves us and will do what He has to do to comfort us so that we are willing to be obedient to Him. Scriptures like Joshua 1:9 are to encourage those who are fearful, discouraged, or disheartened. They are a reminder that God will not call us to something without equipping us. And the best thing He equips us with, is Him!

So here is your reason to praise, you don't have to be afraid to complete any task God has called you to because God Himself is going to be with you wherever you go. That's the word. That's the promise.

If God is calling you to something new, asking you to leave something, or asking you to give up something, you can trust without a doubt that you will find your strength in His promise and can take courage in His leadership. He will not call you to something without preparing you or providing you with all that you need while you are there.

While it might be difficult, there are reasons to praise. It means He trusts you to move forward. It means that you will be walking in His obedient will. It means that you will be able to walk into all of the promises that you have been praying to see manifested.

It takes these transitions of obedience to get you where God has planned to bless you and others.

So if you've been crying over what you are leaving, that's ok. Loss can be difficult. It's okay to mourn because He will comfort you and turn that into joyful dancing. But in the meantime, you must move! You cannot comfortably remain where you are and expect to feel the peace and the joy of the Lord. As you praise let it take you further, you will notice that your latter house will indeed be greater than your former!

Scriptures: Joshua 1:9; Jeremiah 29:11; Hebrews 13:20-21; Ephesians 2:10; Psalm 30:11; Isaiah 61:2; Haggai 2:9

Prayer of Praise: God I thank you that I don't have to be afraid, discouraged, or disheartened by any of the directions you are giving me. I praise you because you promise that I don't have to fear because you are going to be with me wherever I go. I thank you for being an omniscient and omnipresent God. I thank you for fully understanding me and everything around me. I thank you for trusting me to move forward. Thank you for being here with me. Thank you, God! Thank you, God, for giving me yet another reason to praise! In Jesus' name, amen.

Even if it scares you a little bit, what do you feel God is calling you to?

_____

_____

_____

_____

Praise God! Look at how much faith He has in you!

Look at Philippians 1:6 and write it down here:

_____

_____

_____

Does it encourage you? Why or why not?

_____

_____

_____

_____

Still fearful? Or even grateful? Tell God about it:

_____

_____

_____

_____

_____

Write Joshua 1:9 down here:

_____

_____

_____

Is God going to be with you according to the Scripture found in Joshua 1:9?

_____

Repeat and mediate this Scripture until it compels you to move!

Trust God and Praise Him!

Day Thirty-One
He Gave Me Support

Bear one another's burdens, and so fulfill the law of Christ.

-Galatians 6:2

We try to go through far too many things by ourselves! Oh, what a blessing it is to go to God with all of our deepest darkest secrets and know they will not get out if we do something that displeases Him. All of our venting should be with God. He is the greatest ear, comforter, and the only consistent lover of our souls. That's a beautiful reason to praise.

But we must also thank God for bringing certain individuals in our lives that are willing to assist in holding us up as we go through trials, as we walk forward in our purpose, and as we use our gifts for the glory of God.

Many of us have had to deal with people that we trusted and learned the hard way that, maybe we shouldn't have. This makes it very difficult for us to trust people that God brings in our lives to assist us in this part of the journey. I get it! But the reality is, there are just some things you don't have to handle by yourself.

There are times that we need the prayers of the righteous to assist us in pressing through to the next level in God. The word says that the prayers of the righteous work! In James 5:16, it says, they **avail much**. Matter of fact, that whole verse is something awesome but causes many of us to feel afraid. It tells us to confess our trespasses to each other and pray for each other so we may be healed. As I mentioned, a lot of us don't want to be honest about the secret things we deal with because of our own shame and fear of judgment.

But praise God for this verse because it shows that out of all the people on this earth we can't trust there are people that we can! It is possible to pray to God for discernment and wisdom regarding whom we can go to with certain information and even on how much information we share.

If you are going through something God will always be there, His word will always be there for you. But if the burden is far too great and you really can't seem to apply what He is giving you, God will send you someone that can help you through. It's a mandate. We fulfill the law of Christ when we show love to someone, without judgment, by taking their issues straight to God's throne room of grace on their behalf.

Is it easy to do all the time? No. But with prayer and supplication and thanksgiving make your requests known to God, and He will give you peace that surpasses all understanding. As a result of that peace, you will gain clear direction on how to handle what you're going through. And if you need to share so that you can get that help to bear it, He will reveal who that person is.

So praise God that in the midst of storms, it's handled. Also, know that Jesus is interceding (praying) for you at all times. God is so great that He is probably placing you on someone's heart to pray for you right now. They might not have all the details, but they are warring on your behalf praying for your peace and sanity. You're always covered! You just have to believe that and receive the help!

Stay in your word that God may be able to reveal the escapes He has for you to bear the temptations, trials, and storms you face. And trust in God that He will send you all the right help at the right time!

Praise Him!

Scriptures: Galatians 6:2; James 5:16; Hebrews 4:16; Philippians 4:6-7; Romans 8:34

Prayer of Praise: Lord, I thank you that there is always someone out there who can help me bear what I am going through whether they make it known or not. I thank you that you will never leave or forsake me. I thank you that Jesus is making intercession for me. I thank you that you have brought my brothers and sisters in Christ to help support me in the good, the bad, and the ugly. I pray that I will have confidence in this and that when I am in need of help, you will reveal the exact person, you would have me to share with without fear of it getting out. I thank you in advance for that trusted relationship! Thank you, God! Thank you, God, for giving me yet another reason to praise! In Jesus' name, amen.

Whenever I vent recklessly, I find myself thinking, "I shouldn't have said that." So now, I choose to vent to God *first* and allow Him to speak to and deal with my emotional rants. When I've calmed down, I can usually move forward with peace and newfound understanding about me and God.

Read Proverbs 29:11.

I share this Scripture with you not to contradict, but to remind you that venting to God should be your first line of defense. We cannot take things back once we say them, but we can trust that God will not hold these things against us. As it was stated in the devotion, when you go to people with your challenges be led by the Spirit and do so with wisdom.

Do I have friends that I can vent to? Yes, I do! They are a blessing. But I am *slowly* learning that most of what I need to calm me down or make me feel better can be found in the word. That way, I'm taking prayer requests and the important things to my trusted prayer partners and not a jumbled mess of emotions.

If you need to vent to God, take some time and do that right now:

_____
_____
_____
_____
_____
_____
_____
_____
_____

It's hard to trust sometimes, I know, but can you list at least one person that can help you carry your burdens?

_____

_____

If not, write a prayer below asking God to reveal or bring a trustworthy, godly person, in your life!

_____

_____

_____

_____

_____

_____

Before we go, can I give you a few questions to ponder?

Are you someone that can be trusted?

_____

Do you make yourself available to assist in bearing your spiritual brother's and sister's burdens?

_____

How can you improve in this area? *(Because there is always room for improvement)*

_____

_____

_____

It is a blessing when we can be the type of friend that we are asking for. I pray that God will send you these people and that you will continue being that person for someone as well.

Conclusion

I Am a Reason to Praise

In spite of it all, the good, the bad, and the ugly, I am still standing! You are still standing! Even when you feel like you are at your lowest point, I encourage you to look at yourself in the mirror, or your front facing camera, think about all you have been through, and praise Him!

There are many people who have not been able to make it through some of the storms and trials you have been through. There are many people who have not been able to handle God's abundance of blessings like you have.

When you are looking for a reason to praise, just look at yourself. You are a living testimony! You are the epitome of God's grace and an example of the work that Christ can do in the lives of His chosen. You are proof of the perfection in His workmanship. You are proof that His word will not return to Him void, and He will accomplish the very thing He set out to do in you. You are a reason to praise!

What I love most about God and what I will leave you with, is that everything you have been through is not in vain. He will use your story, your bravery, your blessings, to save many alive! You want proof? Let's head over to Genesis 50:20.

But as for you, you meant evil against me; but God meant it for good, in order to bring it about as it is this day, to save many people alive.

Child of God, you are a reason to praise! So praise Him in all things, through all things, and because of all things! He is faithful! We *definitely* have a reason to praise! God bless you! Keep praising! Keep Standing! It's worth it!

Melanie

159

Acknowledgements

Getting this book out of my heart and on the pages took several months of word dumping, countless hours of editing and designing, crazy tear-filled nights and days, and many beautiful souls that helped me on my journey.

Mommy, thank you for allowing me to follow my heart and the call of God on my life. You have helped me in immeasurable ways, and I appreciate the sacrifices you have made for me my whole life, but more specifically, over the last four years. It has been a huge transition for all of us with you being hit pretty hard. But thank you for believing in me. Thank you for not giving up on me or putting me out =).

To the best little brother on earth, my Papabear, thank you for encouraging me in ways only a brother could. Thank you for pulling out and playing that stupid mini violin whenever I complained, pouring into me when I was down, and keeping me laughing when it felt like life was giving me more reasons than ever to cry. Thanks for looking at my designs, helping me with the editing process and pretending like you cared about the things I ranted about. You're the best!

Blakey, thank you for saving my life! You are my angel, joy personified. Thank you for consistently running into my room, jumping on my lap and ruining all the things that I typed trying to find Elmo on my computer. You're my breath of fresh air and one of my heart's inspirations! I love you, nephew!

Daddy, I thank you for seeing the call of God on my life and supporting it. I know I don't say it enough, but I appreciate you, and I love you! Auntie Sharon, thank you for all your prayers, your encouragement, your financial support, your love for me, and the care you take over my gifts and talents. You are appreciated, and I love you! Kim, thank you for believing in me. I know the path I've chosen doesn't always make sense, but you've never discouraged me in following my heart. I thank you for that. To my grandparents, I laugh as I type this thinking of what grandpa would say if I pulled in your garage right now. Even still, thank you for your support with this writing thing. I promise you; it will pay off! Kingdom work always does!

To two of my bests, Arvetta, Lizzy, and my First Lady, Ta'Neisha, thank you! Thank you for seeing more in me than I saw in myself. You believed in this book and those to come in a way that increased my faith in God and myself, and I'm grateful. Thank you for your prayers, the venting sessions, and encouragement.

Pastor Riley, thank you for trusting God enough to trust me with those in your flock. I appreciate you for sharing the hard truths with me, the prophetic words spoken over my life and my gifts, and the encouragement that you provided. You are appreciated!

To Sis. Nona, everyone needs one of you! Thank you for your prayers, your emoji-laden text messages filled with encouragement, and your hugs! I love you! Brother Ronnie, one of my prayer partners, thank you for the talks and the encouragement! I appreciate you! To the Youth and Young Adults of The Neighborhood Church, thank you! Thank you for trusting me, for allowing me to pour into you weekly, but most of all for all that you pour into me. Thank you for encouraging me, challenging me, and believing in me! You guys rock, and I love you!

Shout out to all of you at The Neighborhood Church who have ever encouraged me, laughed with me, fussed at me, prayed with me, and praised with me!

To all of my siblings and family, friends, and my Sessy's (my friends turned sisters) I love you! I thank you! Your support in the good and bad is all I could ever hope for! You're amazing, and I'm blessed to be connected with you all!

Mr. Derek Murphy, thank you for pointing me in the right direction on how to format this book. This would have taken me years to do without you providing me with a starting template! The DIY process wasn't so bad with your help! Thank you for your selflessness, and I pray that God pours back into you fully!

God, thank you for your grace, your patience with me, and for always giving me a reason to praise! You're the real MVP.

Thank you for reading!
Please add a short review on Amazon
and let me know what you thought!

Do you need more encouragement? There is a free six-step eGuide and 10-day devotion eCourse titled, *Encourage Yourself* waiting for you on my website, www.ItsMelanieLee.com.

Struggles are real and so is our ability to fall into a realm of defeat. We don't belong there! So, let *Encourage Yourself* assist you in finding the happy in the midst of *whatever* you're dealing with. Start it today!

www.ItsMelanieLee.Com
www.Facebook.com/ItsMelanieLee
www.Twitter.com/ItsMelanieLee
www.Instagram.com/ItsMelanieLeeIG

Notes

DAY ONE

1. Swanson, James. *Dictionary of Biblical Languages with Semantic Domains:* Hebrew (Old Testament)."Understanding," accessed January, 2016. Oak Harbor: Logos Research Systems, Inc., 1997.

DAY TWENTY-FOUR

1. *Logos Bible Software:* "heart," accessed January, 2016.

Made in the USA
Las Vegas, NV
06 September 2023

77124732R00095